Longman

Biology

11-14

Janet Williams and Chris Workman

Contents

Contents

Contents

Contents

How to use

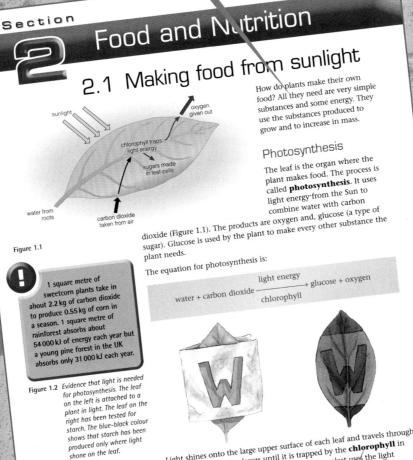

Section 2 — Food and Nutrition

2.1 Making food from sunlight

How do plants make their own food? All they need are very simple substances and some energy. They use the substances produced to grow and to increase in mass.

sunlight

oxygen given out

chlorophyll traps light energy

sugars made in leaf cells

water from roots

carbon dioxide taken from air

Figure 1.1

Photosynthesis

The leaf is the organ where the plant makes food. The process is called **photosynthesis**. It uses light energy from the Sun to combine water with carbon dioxide (Figure 1.1). The products are oxygen and, glucose (a type of sugar). Glucose is used by the plant to make every other substance the plant needs.

The equation for photosynthesis is:

$$\text{water} + \text{carbon dioxide} \xrightarrow[\text{chlorophyll}]{\text{light energy}} \text{glucose} + \text{oxygen}$$

! 1 square metre of sweetcorn plants take in about 2.2 kg of carbon dioxide to produce 0.55 kg of corn in a season. 1 square metre of rainforest absorbs about 54 000 kJ of energy each year but a young pine forest in the UK absorbs only 31 000 kJ each year.

Figure 1.2 Evidence that light is needed for photosynthesis. The leaf on the left is attached to a plant in light. The leaf on the right has been tested for starch. The blue-black colour shows that starch has been produced only where light shone on the leaf.

! Plants only use about 1% of the sunlight reaching the surface of the Earth.

Light shines onto the large upper surface of each leaf and travels through the transparent upper layers until it is trapped by the **chlorophyll** in the chloroplasts of the palisade cells. The chloroplast uses the light energy from the Sun to split water molecules into oxygen and hydrogen. The chloroplast then combines the hydrogen with carbon dioxide to form **sugars**. The first sugar formed is **glucose**. The glucose is then turned into **starch** to be stored for a short time by the leaf cells.

30

Food and nutrition

Summary

○ Plants get their energy from sunlight.

○ Photosynthesis needs chlorophyll to trap th...

○ Photosynthesis combines water with carbo...

○ Glucose and oxygen are produced by phot...

○ Glucose can be used to make starch, cellul...

Questions

1 Copy and complete the following sentences. Plants make their own food using _____ energy, carbon dioxide from the air and _____ from the soil. The process is called _____. _____ (e.g. glucose) is produced and used to make all other substances the plant needs. _____ is a waste product. Leaves look _____ because they contain chlorophyll. The _____ traps the light energy. Most chlorophyll is in the _____ cells near the top surface of a leaf. [Total 4

2 Give two functions of the roots of a plant. [Total 2

3 List the raw materials and substances needed for photosynthesis. In a second column state where the plant gets the substance from. [Total 8

4 List the first products from photosynthesis. In a second column state where the substance goes to when it moves out of the chloroplast. [Total 4

5 Name five substances that plants make from the glucose produced in photosynthesis. [Total 5

6 A shoot of pondweed was placed in a boiling tube of pond water. A bench lamp with a 60 W bulb shining on the tube was placed 20 cm away. An oxygen probe was

Summary boxes: Each chapter ends with a summary which will help you to draw together what you have just read. They will also help you revise.

y.

nlight energy.

nicals.

into the tube and the oxygen concentration
orded by a data-logger. The oxygen concentration
s recorded after four minutes and again after a
ther five minutes. The experiment was repeated with
same pondweed but with the lamp 5 cm away from
boiling tube. The results are given in Table 1.1.

e of m)	Oxygen concentration after 4 min (% saturation)	Oxygen concentration after 9 min (% saturation)
	60	65
	64	84

Work out the increase in oxygen percentage
per minute from the pondweed at 20 cm
and 5 cm lamp distances. [2]
What is the effect of increasing the light
on oxygen production. [1]
State the name of the process that
produces the oxygen. [1]
Explain, in as much detail as you can, why the
amount of oxygen produced in this experiment
increased when the lamp was put closer to
the pondweed. [4]
The lamp also gives off heat. Suggest how this
could affect the results. [2]
[Total 10]

Applications

Biosurgery: nature's healers

In the twentieth century antibiotics were used a great deal to treat
wounds. But in the past maggots were used instead. Maggots were
used by the Aborigines of Australia, the hill people of Burma,
Europeans, and the Mayans of South America to treat wounds.

A surgeon, Baron Dominique-Jean Larrey, serving with Napoleon in
the 1820s invented the field ambulance. He recorded in his diary how
soldiers with maggot infested wounds would arrive at his tents already
showing signs of recovery. William Baer, a surgeon in World War I,
described a situation where he saw two soldiers on the battlefield who
had maggots in their wounds for several days, but these men had no
fever or infection. The maggots were protecting the soldiers from
diseases such as tetanus and septicaemia and at the same time healing
their wounds by eating the rotting tissue.

After World War I, in 1929, Baer began trials using blowfly maggots to
treat wounds. His results were very good. He then began to cultivate
blowflies to use their eggs. By the 1930s maggot therapy, as it was
called, was also being used in Canada and the USA in more than 300
hospitals. With the discovery of antibiotics, by the end of World War
II, penicillin was used on a large scale to treat wounds. Maggot therapy
virtually disappeared.

Figure 1 *Maggots cleaning a wound.*

In the 1980s and 1990s it has been found that bacteria are becoming
increasingly resistant to antibiotics. Super-bugs such as methicillin
resistant *Staphylococcus aureus* (MRSA) are causing severe problems
preventing wounds from healing. Maggots can achieve naturally what
artificial medicines are failing to do. In 1990, an American doctor,
Robert Sherman, noticed healthy infection-free tissue in a leg wound
crawling with maggots. He set up an insectary to breed maggots for use
in hospitals in California. He conducted trials and showed that larva
therapy, as it is now called, increases the rate of healing of pressure
sores. It is also more cost effective than treatment with surgery and
antibiotics. Although maggot therapy is effective many health
professionals are reluctant to use the method.

Maggots are not the only creatures to be used in biosurgery. Leeches
are also used. Leeches have suckers that suck blood. They were used as
early as 200 BC for the purpose of blood letting by healers. By the
nineteenth century this practice had become unfashionable.

Figure 2 *The saliva of leeches improves blood circulation*

**History and Applications
pages:** At the end of each section
there is a double page that looks
at the history of science. Each
topic on these pages is linked to
part of the work in the section
you have just read. There is also a
double page that looks at the
ways that science can be applied
to everyday things.

Question boxes: There are question boxes at the end of each chapter
and each section. The questions towards the end of each box may be a
little harder, to help you to see how well you have understood the work.

Some questions have an **R** next to them. These are research questions.
You will need to use other books or the Internet to write a full answer to
these questions.

In the end of section questions some questions have a **P** next to them.
These questions can be used to help you plan practical investigations.

Cells and life processes

1.1 Characteristics of living things

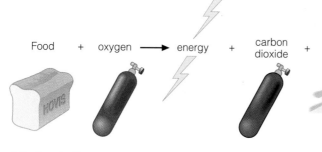

Figure 1.1

What is an **organism**? The term is used to describe a separate object which carries out living processes. There are about two million different types of organisms.

How can you tell if something is living or dead? Is a robot alive? Several questions need to be asked about the organism or object. There are seven **characteristics** of living things. If something does all seven of these over its lifetime then it is living.

The seven key characteristics of living things are:

Movement. This is a change of position needed to respond to the surroundings. Animals move their whole body from place to place but plants can only move parts of their body.

Figure 1.2 *Movement.*

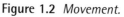

Food + oxygen → energy + carbon dioxide + water

Figure 1.3 *Respiration.*

Respiration. This is the release of energy from food or stored chemicals in cells for immediate use by the organism.

Sensitivity. Individuals need information from the environment to react and carry out the other living processes. They respond to different stimuli. Plants will grow in the direction light is coming from and animals may move in response to seeing something coming towards them.

Figure 1.4 *Sensitivity.*

Figure 1.5 *Growth.*

Figure 1.6 *Reproduction.*

Growth. Individuals start off small and grow until 'adulthood'. Animals often have a maximum size but plants continue to get bigger over all of their life.

Reproduction. This creates new individuals. They replace those that have died and ensure the survival of the species.

Excretion. This is the removal of waste produced by chemical reactions in cells of the individual. This includes gases (carbon dioxide), special compounds (urea) and water. Plants excrete toxins into their leaves. They then drop the leaves in autumn.

Nutrition (feeding). The organism must take in energy to keep it alive. Plants take in simple compounds and light to make their own chemicals. Animals eat plants or other animals to get complex compounds from them.

Figure 1.8 *Nutrition*

Figure 1.7 *Excretion.*

These seven points are often remembered by a mnemonic, e.g. MRS GREN. Can you think of another mnemonic that is special to you and your friends?

Can you work out if a car is alive? It can move from place to place, it feeds on petrol, takes in oxygen and gives out waste substances. Its engine burns fuel and some cars can react to the environment by turning on lights if it is dark. However it does not grow or reproduce. It cannot be alive.

The male Emperor moth can detect the scent of a female from up to 11 km away. The chemoreceptors on the male antennae can detect single molecules of the scent.

A camel's hump is full of fat, not water. Camels combine the fat with oxygen to release energy and water is made too.

The list of processes shows that there are differences between plants and animals. This is because of the way they feed. A plant must trap enough light energy from the sun by spreading out its leaves over a large area. Movement is not necessary for this form of nutrition, unlike typical animal nutrition. A comparison of the features of animals and plants is in Table 1.1.

Animals	Plants
Move whole of the body from place to place.	Only move parts of the plant.
Compact structure.	Branching structure with large surface area for both leaves and roots.
Usually grows to a maximum size.	Grows throughout its life.
Variety of colours.	Leaves usually green.
Respond to stimuli quickly.	Respond to stimuli slowly.
Complex behaviour patterns.	Very simple behaviour.
Most animals reproduce by adult moving to find another adult.	Reproduce by pollen being moved by some agent (e.g. wind) to reach the ovule of another individual plant.
Young move away from parents by their own movement.	Young (seeds) spread by another organism or the wind.

Table 1.1 *A comparison of the features of animals and plants.*

The differences between familiar large organisms should be obvious to you but what happens to living things that are too small to see? Usually they are more similar to animals than plants. However, because they are so small, air or water currents may move them from place to place. The micro-organisms only grow a small amount so they usually reproduce quickly by dividing into two. A large group of them seen together is called a colony. Also, because they are so small, they don't need much food and can absorb what they need through their surface. The disadvantage of being small is that larger organisms will eat them!

Summary

- There are about two million different types of living things.
- Living things are described by seven life processes (MRS GREN).
- Animals and plants differ because of the way they get their food.

Questions

1 Copy and complete the following sentences. Animals can _____ from place to place but plants only move part of their bodies. The release of energy inside cells is called _____. Sensitivity is important for organisms so that they can _____ to the stimuli. Organisms increase in size when they _____. Sexual reproduction requires two _____ and special sex cells. Some plants can _____ from one parent, e.g. when a new plant develops from a cutting. Waste produced by the cells of the organism must be removed. This is called _____. Carbon dioxide, water and urine are examples of animal _____. _____ get rid of poisons when they drop their _____. _____ feed on other organisms but plants can feed on non-living substances. The intake of the food is called _____. *[Total 6]*

2 Copy out and match up the life process with the correct description.

respiration   change of position of part or whole of organism

nutrition   production of new individuals

movement   removal of waste products

reproduction   intake of chemicals for energy and growth

excretion   the release of energy in cells

[Total 5]

3 List three things that are excreted from an animal and one that is excreted from a plant. *[Total 4]*

4 Explain how each of the following get their food:
a) micro-organisms (bacteria)   *[2]*
b) plants   *[2]*
c) animals.   *[1]*
[Total 5]

5 Suggest two substances or items that you think are similar to living things but do not fit all of the seven criteria. *[Total 2]*

6 An alien landed on earth and tried to work out if a washing machine was alive. What questions should it ask to find out if it is living? *[Total 7]*

7 Describe the main difference in shape between animals and plants and explain how the shape helps the organism to live. *[Total 4]*

1.2 Where organisms live

How are organisms adapted to the place they live? A polar bear could not live in a hot desert because it would get too hot. A fish cannot live out of water because it cannot get oxygen from the air. Each type of organism is able to live in one kind of environment.

Habitats

Figure 2.1 *A deciduous woodland habitat.*

To us the earth is a very special place. Life may have started about 3500 million years ago and organisms are now able to live in most areas of the sea, land or air. Very few areas are entirely free of life. The surface of the earth where living things can survive is called the **biosphere**.

Organisms live in specific places in the biosphere. The place where each organism can live is called its **habitat**. This is a local **environment** which usually describes the main type of plant or the structure of the environment e.g. a woodland, a pond, the seashore. The organism must be adapted to the special conditions existing in that area. Different species (types of organisms) will each be **adapted** to that particular habitat and form an interacting group – a **community** of organisms.

The organisms interact with the non-living environment. The combination of the community of organisms and the non-living (physical) environment is called the **ecosystem**. Ecosystems are often grouped together on a global scale to give **biomes** (Figure 2.2). These are large areas where similar types of plants can grow.

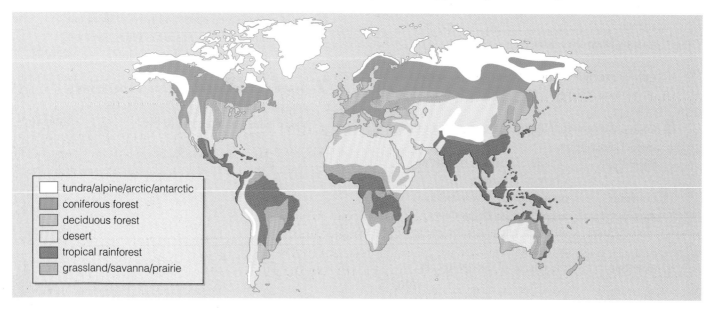

tundra/alpine/arctic/antarctic
coniferous forest
deciduous forest
desert
tropical rainforest
grassland/savanna/prairie

Figure 2.2 *The major biomes of the world.*

Adaptations

Each organism is adapted to live in the habitat where it is found. The adaptations often appear strange to us but are essential to the organism. In the sea, a blue whale has tail flukes to help it move through the oceans, with small arms (seen as flippers) to help direct the whale in the water. It feeds by filtering the sea water for small organisms which it swallows using its strong tongue. Its nostril (blowhole) is on the top of its head to allow breathing when swimming at the surface. It also has a special blood circulation system to ensure that the brain and heart muscle have the best oxygen supply to conserve 'air' during a long dive.

Figure 2.3 *Blue whale.*

Some cactus plants look like spiky balls instead of a 'normal' plant, but this helps them to survive in the desert. Spines are present to protect the cactus from animals eating it. There are no leaves and only the green ribbed stem is used to capture sunlight.

The ribs create some areas of shade so that carbon dioxide can enter for photosynthesis without the cactus losing too much water. The stem has a small surface area which cuts down water loss. The roots are usually long and spread over a wide area so that if it rains water can be absorbed quickly and stored within the stem.

These are just two examples of the ways organisms can be adapted to the physical environment. Some organisms need to change during the day and throughout the year to take advantage of the different conditions.

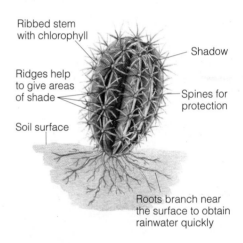
Ribbed stem with chlorophyll
Shadow
Ridges help to give areas of shade
Spines for protection
Soil surface
Roots branch near the surface to obtain rainwater quickly

Figure 2.4 *Sea urchin cactus.*

Daily changes

Organisms respond to the daily changes in physical factors to maximise their survival in the habitat. A crocus plant will open its flower in bright sunshine when it is most likely to be warm enough for insects to fly so that they can pollinate the flower. In sunlight, leaves will also open small pores (holes) on the surface so that carbon dioxide can be taken in for photosynthesis. Later in the day, when the light is less bright, the pores close to stop water loss.

Different organisms are active at different times of the day so that they can protect themselves from predators and gather enough food. For example, a bat has a better chance of catching insects at night when it can sense them but it cannot be seen. During the day the bat must hide in its roost to avoid its own predators.

> **!** Zoos help to breed endangered species so that they do not become extinct. Sometimes they can release the individuals back into the wild. For example, red kites have been released in North Wales and red-crowned cranes in Japan and north-east China.

Seasonal changes

In an oak wood you can see how the organisms have adapted to the seasons. The oak trees burst into leaf in late spring so that they gain the maximum amount of sunshine in the warmest conditions. Underneath the oak trees, holly trees have very thick dark green leaves to absorb as much light as possible in the shade of the bigger trees above.

Squirrels are active during the day as they need light to collect their food. At night they defend themselves by resting and hiding from the nocturnal predators in the wood. The squirrels remain active all summer and find enough food to raise a family.

As autumn approaches wood mice store more of their food energy as fat to last them through the winter. When the air temperature falls the wood mouse's respiration slows down and its body temperature decreases. It **hibernates** to save energy during the cold months.

The oak tree loses its leaves to make sure that the branches are not damaged by stronger winds and so that the delicate leaves are not damaged by frost. Another advantage to the oak tree is that waste chemicals can also be lost from the tree in the falling leaves. The smaller holly tree can now receive more light and so continues to grow slowly using its better-protected leaves.

In spring, as the temperature increases again but before the oak leaves open, bluebells grow using food stored in their bulbs. They flower early so that the insects and wind can get to the flowers without hindrance from the oak tree leaves. The leaves of the bluebell use the light energy getting to the woodland floor to create a new bulb for the next year ... and so on for many years.

The flowers of the bluebell are adapted to attract insects. They are colourful and perfumed. Insects arrive to get food as a reward but they also carry the pollen from one flower to the next. Each flower must only give the insect a small amount of food so that it will fly to another flower instead of going to the hive or nest. The flower and the insect developed together millions of years ago. The insect cannot live without the flowers and the flowers cannot reproduce without the insects. This is an example of co-evolution and the beneficial way organisms can interact within a community.

> **!** Spiders and insects are among the oldest types of animals on the earth – about 300 million years old.

Figure 2.5 *Insect pollinating a bluebell.*

Summary

- The biosphere is divided into biomes.
- An ecosystem consists of the non-living environment and living organisms.
- A habitat is the place where an individual organism lives.
- The group of organisms living in a habitat is a community.
- Organisms are adapted to the habitat in which they live.
- Daily and seasonal changes occur in the habitat. Organisms respond to these changes.

Questions

1 Copy and complete the following sentences.
The surface of the earth where living things can survive is called the _____. The organisms can only live in the areas to which they are suited. The area that one type of organism is found in is called the _____. Several different types of organism living together is called a _____.
The physical parts of the habitat, e.g. light, wind, temperature, and the community of organisms make up the _____. *[Total 2]*

2 What is the biosphere? *[Total 1]*

3 Explain the difference between a community and an ecosystem. *[Total 2]*

4 Describe how a cactus is adapted to prevent it losing water. *[Total 3]*

5 Suggest how an oak tree survives conditions in winter. *[Total 2]*

6 Explain why a flower produces only a small amount of nectar (food for insects) at a time. *[Total 2]*

7 An investigation into where woodlice live used a chamber where half was damp and half dry. The 20 woodlice in the chamber could move freely between the areas. After 10 minutes in the chamber 16 woodlice were in the damp area and 4 in the dry.
a) Calculate the percentage of woodlice in the damp area. *[1]*
b) Why do you think more woodlice were in the damp area? *[1]*
c) The surface of a woodlouse allows water to pass through easily. Why is it important to stay in a damp area? *[1]*
d) If a woodlouse stayed in a dry atmosphere for several hours, what would happen to the mass of the animal? Try to explain why. *[2]*
e) What type of habitat is the most likely place for you to find woodlice? *[2]*
[Total 7]

1.3 Organs

How does an organism allow all of the different life processes to go on at the same time? An individual or organism must be complex to carry out all of the living processes needed to survive. Each process (do you remember MRS GREN?) is carried out in a different region of the body.

Imagine if everyone in your class tried to do their favourite subject at the same time in the same place. Trying to do a biology experiment next to someone speaking French and someone else kicking a ball around the room is not very efficient. Each activity may get done but they interfere with each other. The school's answer is to create special areas for different studies and to co-ordinate the movement of pupils between the areas. Plants and animals are co-ordinated in the same way.

The body is divided into **organs**. Each carries out one major function. The organs are often arranged into **organ systems** so that several associated functions are co-ordinated. The product of one activity can be passed directly onto another for further treatment. The activities are controlled by the body itself. For example, if you smell food you produce saliva so that you can start to break up the food and swallow it. The saliva helps the food get to your stomach. In the stomach, the food is changed again. The use of energy in the body is much more efficient if each job is done in many small steps.

In mammals and plants the following are the major organ systems associated with the life processes previously described.

Digestive system

The digestive system takes in, breaks down, and absorbs the soluble products in food and removes undigested food. This is the way all energy and nutrients enter the body. The only equivalent in plants is for the root to absorb water and nutrients.

Breathing system

This consists of the organs associated with breathing and gas exchange to supply oxygen for respiration and to remove carbon dioxide, e.g. lungs in mammals, gills in fish. The leaves of plants have the same function.

Circulation system

This transports all soluble materials around the body. The heart pumps the blood which circulates in blood vessels. Plants move water and chemicals through vascular bundles (veins) in the stem and leaves.

Excretory system

Waste produced by the cells is removed from the body. Excretion usually refers to the removal of urine by the kidneys but should also include the lungs and skin as organs that get rid of waste gas or substances. Plants remove waste when they lose their leaves.

Nervous system

This controls the organism's response to stimuli. It includes the sense organs, brain and nerves. In plants there is no equivalent but there are sensitive regions, e.g. tips of shoots are sensitive to light.

Skeletal system

Made up of bones and muscles for support and movement. The bones can also protect the body. In plants the vascular bundles have supporting tissue next to them. Plant cells use water and the cell wall to support them.

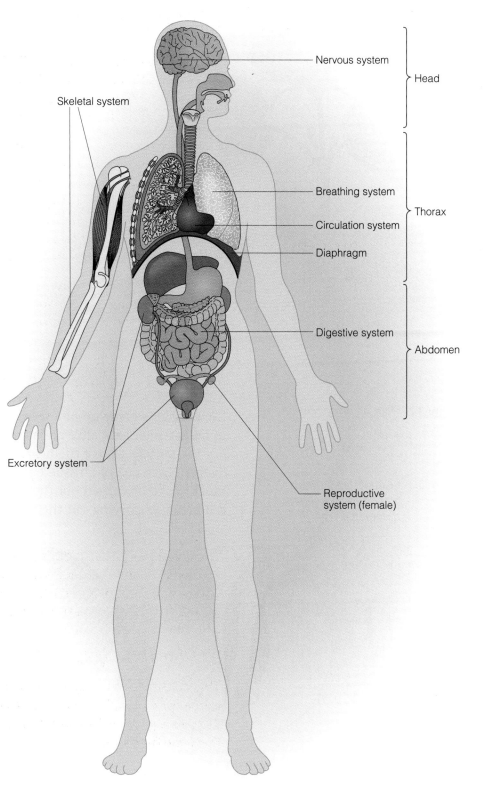

Figure 3.1 *Human organ systems.*

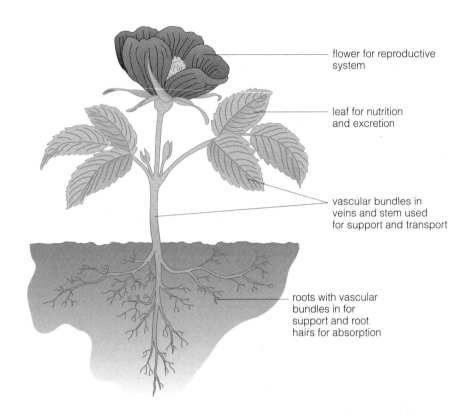

flower for reproductive system

leaf for nutrition and excretion

vascular bundles in veins and stem used for support and transport

roots with vascular bundles in for support and root hairs for absorption

Reproductive system

Organs associated with production of sex cells and development of the young. Male organs are different from female and are in different individuals for animals. In plants both sex structures are in the flowers.

Figure 3.2 *Plant organ systems.*

Figure 3.3 *Relationship between organ systems, organs, tissues and cells.*

Each organ is made up of a series of tissues. The **tissues** are groups of **cells** which look alike and carry out a single function in the organ e.g. the muscle cells of the heart contract but the blood cells carry the oxygen. Each cell of a tissue has a similar structure. For the different functions to be carried out the cells must be specialised. This makes the cell better at carrying out the task.

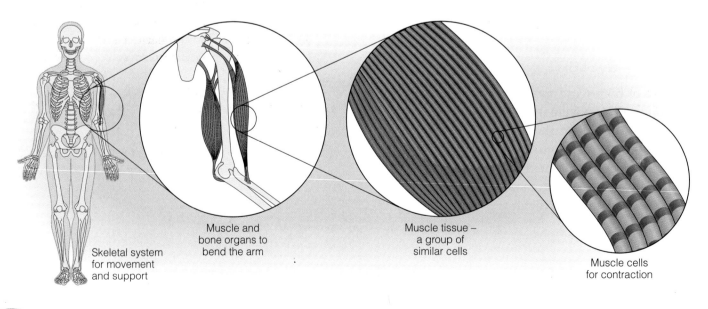

Skeletal system for movement and support

Muscle and bone organs to bend the arm

Muscle tissue – a group of similar cells

Muscle cells for contraction

Summary

- A tissue is a group of similar cells.
- An organ is made up of tissues, each of which carry out a particular function.
- Organs are grouped into organ systems to make the functions more efficient.
- The body of a mammal is divided into the head, thorax and abdomen.

Questions

1 Copy and complete the following sentences. Organ systems are a series of _____ carrying out related activities so that one overall function is done more efficiently. The substances _____ from one organ can be used by the next to complete the function of the organ _____. The organs are made from groups of similar cells called a _____. *[Total 2]*

2 Place the following items in order of increasing size:
digestive system   organism
cell   stomach   muscle tissue   *[Total 1]*

3 What are the functions of the following organs:
a) flower   *[1]*
b) root   *[1]*
c) heart   *[1]*
d) skeleton   *[1]*
e) lungs?   *[1]*
     [Total 5]

4 Which organs are involved in the following processes? There may be more than one for each process. Include plants where applicable.
a) excretion of urea   *[1]*
b) thinking   *[1]*
c) movement   *[2]*
d) absorbing energy into the 'body'.   *[3]*
     [Total 7]

5 Explain why organs are arranged into organ systems.   *[Total 2]*

6 The human chest is also known as the thorax.
a) What divides it from the abdomen?   *[1]*
b) Make a table to list the organs in each of the head, thorax, abdomen and limbs.   *[Total 13]*

7 Describe how the digestive system does some of the opposite jobs to the excretory system.   *[Total 2]*

1.4 Cells

What is a cell? In 1665 Robert Hooke used a microscope to examine cork from an oak tree. He saw tiny boxes similar to a monk's cell (which is a small room) so he named the structures 'cells'. All living things are made up of these cells but what is inside them?

Cell structure

An organism is made up of **cells**. It is really like a house made of different components such as bricks, wood and glass. Each small component is arranged in a special way, and carries out a particular job, so that the house becomes a complete functioning unit. All the cells have the same overall structure that allows them to carry out the basic life processes but some are changed to carry out special functions. All cells have the following structures.

● The **cell membrane** surrounds the cell. It is very thin and cannot be seen using a light microscope. It holds the substances in the cell and acts as a 'gatekeeper' to control the chemicals that can enter or leave. The membrane is flexible and will fold or bend but if too much strain is put onto it the membrane will break and the cell dies.

● Inside the cell membrane is a soup of chemicals and complex structures which carry out all of the activities of the cell. It is called the **cytoplasm** and is usually seen under the light microscope to have granules in it. These are **organelles**, specialised areas of the cell where particular jobs are carried out. The granules can also be small **vesicles** which store food reserves or break down unwanted substances. The cytoplasm is colourless but the consistency can vary from a thick gel to runny. In some cells, like the pond organism *Amoeba*, different regions of the cytoplasm have different consistencies.

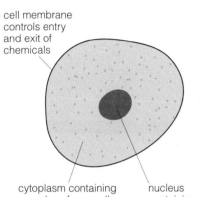

cell membrane controls entry and exit of chemicals

cytoplasm containing granules of organelles and vesicles

nucleus containing information to control the cell

Figure 4.1 *An animal cell.*

Figure 4.2 *Human cheek cells (flattened epithelial cells) stained with methylene blue and magnified 200 times. Note the light blue coloured nucleus, granular cytoplasm and folded edges. They are very thin cells. Several layers of the cells make up the inside of the cheek surface.*

● Each cell has a **nucleus**, to control the activities of the cell. It stores all the information in coded form in molecules of **DNA** (deoxyribonucleic acid) found in the **chromosomes**. Relevant parts of the code are copied and then sent to the cytoplasm. There it is decoded so that the required action is carried out. For example, milk must be made in the mammary gland cell so the codes for milk production are sent to the cytoplasm to make it.

Plant cells

Both plant and animal cells have all the three features described already but plant cells have extra features.

● The **cell wall** is made by the plant cell from a special chemical called **cellulose**. This chemical has long fibres and is very strong. It forms a wall on the outside of the cell membrane to support the cell and stop the contents bursting when it is full of water. It is quite thick and can easily be seen through a light microscope. The plant cells appear to be separated from each other. The cell wall allows substances to pass between the fibres so that they can enter or leave the cell freely.

● The **permanent vacuole** is a bag-like structure containing a dilute solution. It is seen in the middle of the cytoplasm. Its functions include the storage of waste substances, or giving colour to the cells e.g. the red of beetroot. It will also take in water from the surroundings of the cell to create a pressure against the cell wall. This is like a football when it is blown up or a fizzy drink bottle when it is shaken. The cell becomes very firm and is able to support the plant without a hard skeleton. The permanent vacuole is separated from the cytoplasm by a membrane similar to the one surrounding the cell.

● **Chloroplasts** are the structures that contain the green pigment chlorophyll. They are not found in every plant cell but there are many in leaf cells. They are seen as small green dots in the cytoplasm of the cells. They trap light energy to make food for the plant. They are separated from the cytoplasm by a membrane but chemicals can move between the two very easily.

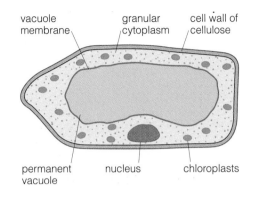

vacuole membrane   granular cytoplasm   cell wall of cellulose

permanent vacuole   nucleus   chloroplasts

Figure 4.3 *A plant cell.*

Figure 4.4 *The epidermal cells are separated by cellulose cell walls. The nucleus is at the side of the cells. No vacuole can be seen as there is no coloured substance in it. The cytoplasm looks rough due to the different organelles and storage substances. There are no chloroplasts as the cells are from inside the onion bulb.*

! A fully grown human has about 100 million million cells. If each cell is 0.02 mm long, a single line of the cells would stretch 200 000 km or five times around the world.

Why are plant and animal cells different?

An animal needs to move from place to place to catch its food so it needs to be light. Some of the cells must also bend (muscle cells get shorter and fatter) so that the organism can move. The animal must have some sort of rigid skeleton to attach its muscles to and give it the required shape but individual cells do not need support which would be heavy. Therefore the cells are very weak because they do not have a cell wall. They have a simple basic plan but can be modified to carry out specialised functions. Animal cells need to absorb simple but ready made chemicals as their food.

On the other hand a plant needs only to stay still and have a large surface area to trap sunlight energy. It has cells that are supported by the cell wall so a skeleton is not needed. As long as there is enough water in the cells the plant stands upright. The chloroplasts trap the light energy and the cells can use the stored energy directly.

Animal cells	Plant cells
nucleus present	nucleus present
cell membrane	cell membrane
cytoplasm	cytoplasm
no chloroplasts	chloroplasts often present
no cell wall	cell wall made of cellulose
only temporary vacuoles	permanent sap vacuole
variety of shapes	regular boxes in appearance
usually smaller	usually larger
food stored mainly as glycogen*	food stored mainly as starch

Table 4.1 *Similarities and differences between cells. (* glycogen is made of glucose molecules packed tightly together in a particular way)*

Unicellular organisms

Animals and plants are made up of many cells. They are **multicellular**. However they are not the only types of organism. Others are single-celled (**unicellular**). Some unicellular organisms have a nucleus surrounded by a nuclear membrane (like the nucleus in an animal or plant cell). There are also organisms with a very simple structure. These include bacteria. They are different because the DNA is in the cytoplasm and not in a separate nucleus. Scientists think that they were the first types of cells to evolve.

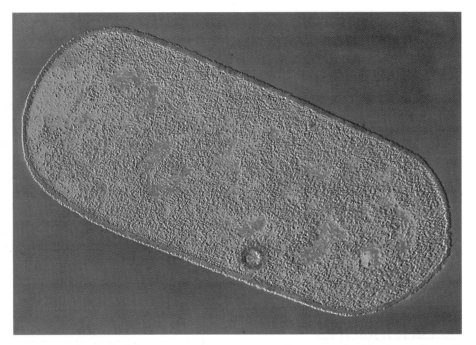

Figure 4.5 *Bacillus bacterium cell.*

Bacteria show this type of structure. They are very small (less than 0.002 mm long). They do not have a nucleus but there is a single circular chromosome which controls the activities of the cell. Some of them have fine hairs sticking out called flagella which help the cells to move. They divide into two to reproduce. This can be done as often as every 20 minutes so the numbers increase very quickly.

 Most bacteria are not harmful to humans, but, during the Great Plague of 1665, (which was caused by bacteria carried by fleas) 68 956 people died from plague in London alone.

Bacterial cells	Animal and Plant cells
no separate nucleus	have a distinct nucleus surrounded by a nuclear membrane
single chromosome made only of DNA	several chromosomes made of DNA and other chemicals
no organelles bound by membranes	separate organelles in the cytoplasm
usually smaller than 0.002 mm	usually larger than 0.010 mm

Table 4.2 *Differences between bacterial and animal and plant cells.*

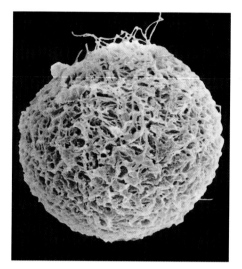

Figure 5.2 *Sperm cells surrounding an ovum.*

Sex cells (**gametes**) must also be specialised because they must fuse together to form a new individual. This means that they must have half the normal number of chromosomes in each nucleus. When a **sperm** fertilises an **ovum** the normal number is restored and the new cell can divide to produce all the other cells in the organism. The sperm must be able to swim to the ovum so it has a tail (this is a large cilium called a flagellum). The sperm also has lots of energy-releasing organelles at the junction between the head and tail to power the tail. The ovum is much larger than the sperm because there needs to be a large amount of food stored for a fertilised egg to use when it develops.

Red blood cells do not have a nucleus. This is so that there is more room for the molecule **haemoglobin** to carry oxygen. Their biconcave disc shape allows red blood cells to be flexible so they can be pushed through the narrowest blood vessels. Their shape also gives them a large surface area for gas exchange.

White blood cells do have a nucleus and some can change shape to squeeze between other cells and also to move around a foreign object or cell (e.g. bacterium) and engulf it. The cytoplasm then digests the foreign object. This is one way that an animal can defend itself against disease (see Section 3, chapter 3).

Figure 5.3 *Scanning electron micrograph of red and white blood cells. The red blood cells are thinner in the middle (biconcave). The white blood cells look yellow in this micrograph.*

Nerve cells are specialised to carry electrical impulses. They are very long so the impulse is carried over a large distance without interruption. The branched ends of a nerve cell allow many connections to other nerve cells so that the impulse can be co-ordinated.

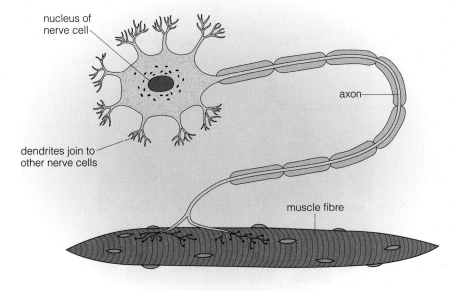

nucleus of nerve cell

axon

dendrites join to other nerve cells

muscle fibre

Figure 5.4 *The nerve cell carries an impulse to make the muscle cells contract.*

The muscle cell is also long to help it contract further. It has proteins in the cytoplasm which can slide over each other so the cell contracts. There are many organelles to release the energy needed for contraction.

Plant cell specialisms

The **palisade** cells have many chloroplasts to capture light energy for the leaf to make the food for the plant (Figure 5.5). The cell wall and other parts of the cytoplasm are transparent to let the light through. The oblong shape allows many of the cells to pack closely together at the top of the leaf so that as much light as possible is trapped. Palisade cells use the light energy to turn carbon dioxide and water into glucose and oxygen.

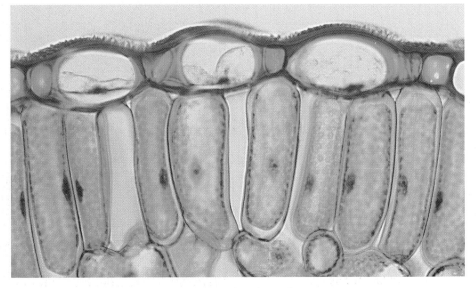

Figure 5.5 *Leaf palisade cells showing many chloroplasts.*

The surface area of a **root hair cell** is increased by the 'hair' so that more water can be absorbed into the root. There are no chloroplasts or storage structures so the cells are transparent and seem to lack structure. However, they have organelles to release energy so that some mineral salts can be actively absorbed into the cell from the soil.

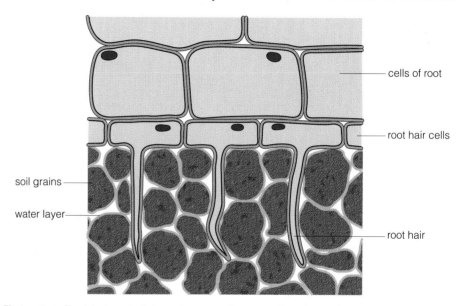

cells of root

root hair cells

soil grains

water layer

root hair

Figure 5.6 *Root hair cells have a large surface area for absorption.*

In plants, water is carried in long thin hollow tubes called **xylem vessels**. The vessels are formed from a column of cells but the end walls, cytoplasm and nucleus have all been destroyed. The water can flow freely from one 'cell' to the next.

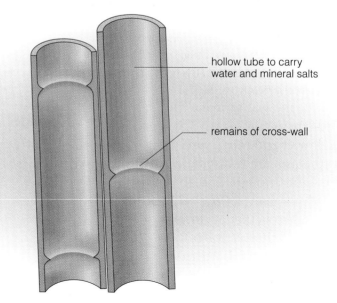

hollow tube to carry water and mineral salts

remains of cross-wall

Figure 5.7 *Xylem vessels have no end walls, cytoplasm or nucleus.*

Summary

○ An organism is made of organs, each having many tissues.

○ The cells of most tissues in an organism are specialised.

○ Specialisms allow each cell to carry out its function more efficiently.

○ The structure of a cell indicates the type of function it does.

Questions

1 Copy and complete the following sentences.
Cells differ from each other so that they can do different _____. A _____ _____ cell has fine hairs (cilia) which are waved in a rhythm so that mucus can be moved. Sperm cells have a whip-like _____ to move them through a liquid. Red blood cells do not have a nucleus but the _____ has lots of haemoglobin to carry more oxygen. _____ cells are long to carry impulses quickly from one place to another. Plant cells like _____ hair cells have a long projection to increase the surface area for absorption of water. _____ cells are hollow tubes to let the water flow easily through them. All of these adaptations make the cells better at carrying out their function. *[Total 4]*

2 Explain, with as much detail as you can, how bacteria are moved out of the lungs. *[Total 3]*

3 How is a ciliated epithelial cell different from a squamous epithelial cell (lining cell of the cheek)? (Hint: See p14) *[Total 2]*

4 State similarities and differences between red blood cells and xylem vessels. *[Total 6]*

5 Describe how a palisade cell is adapted to make food for the plant. *[Total 3]*

6 What are the advantages of cells being specialised? *[Total 2]*

7 Suggest two reasons why there are more types of animal cell than plant cell. *[Total 2]*

History

Microscopes and cells

A good scientist asks questions and makes observations. Sometimes the questions are too difficult to be answered by the equipment available at the time. The ideas and evidence often develop together.

In 1665, Robert Hooke was trying to answer an intriguing question. What was living matter made up from? The development of microscopes to view living material started in 1608 when Zacharias Jansen developed a system of putting two lenses in sequence to give greater magnification than with a single lens. Unfortunately the quality of the lenses was poor and the image produced did not really help investigation of the minute world.

Galileo made improvements to microscope design (about 1610) and by 1660 simple microscopes were able to help Malpighi provide the evidence that blood went from arteries to veins through tiny vessels called capillaries. He had studied the lungs of a frog to come to this conclusion.

Five years later, when Charles II was king and England was suffering from the plague, Robert Hooke used a basic compound microscope of three lenses. He had to cut a very thin section of the soft cork tissue found under the bark of trees. The thin layer was put onto a black surface under the microscope and, with the light angled in the correct direction, he saw a series of pores like a honeycomb. The pores were not all the same size or shape. He interpreted them as boxes and called them 'cells'.

The amateur Dutch technologist Anton van Leeuwenhoek used a system of a single lens that gave a clearer image. He described what we now know as bacteria, protozoa, sperm and blood cells in about 1670.

The evidence of tiny units making up all organisms was not accepted until there was some way of showing they could reproduce.

More than one hundred years later Robert Brown (1773–1853) used a better series of lenses to identify a spot in all the cells of plants and animals. He called this the nucleus. Further studies by Matthias Schleiden (in 1838) and Theodor Schwann (in 1839) showed that the nucleus divided into two when more cells were produced. They put forward the idea that all tissues of plants and animals were made of cells.

Theordor Boveri (1887) went further by accurately describing coloured bodies (chromosomes) in the nucleus when the cell divided. Using sea urchin eggs and sperm he worked out the importance of the chromosomes to control the development of the cell and, from it, the whole organism.

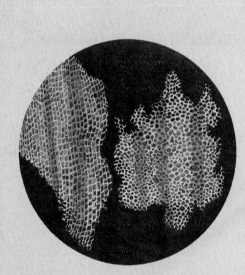

Figure 1 *Robert Hooke's drawing of cork cells.*

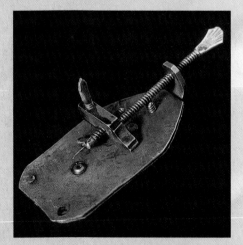

Figure 2 *Leeuwenhoek's microscope. The lens is mounted in a hole in the metal plate and the object moved by 2 screws next to the lens.*

The system for looking at small structures was now at its limit because it used light to see the objects. The smallest structure that could be looked at was about 0.0005 mm. Smaller parts of the cells were not seen until the development of the electron microscope.

In the 1930s various people, including James Hillier, developed the idea that electrons could be used instead of light in microscopes. Hillier managed a magnification of 7000 times with his electron microscope. Commercial electron microscopes were first made in Germany (Siemens, 1939). A detailed investigation of parts of cells needed thinner sections so different systems of preparing the tissues were developed. It is now possible to see objects as small as 0.000 001 mm (1 nanometre). In the mid 1950s the structures inside cells were described for the first time e.g. membranes and ribosomes. Using knowledge of the structures, scientists started to understand the processes going on inside cells.

Three-dimensional images of the surfaces of structures can be seen using a scanning electron microscope. A scanning tunnelling electron microscope, developed in 1981 by Gerd Binnig and Heinrich Rohrer, is able to view the surface of molecules and atoms. This complements computer modelling of molecules to understand the interactions between them. Molecular biology is an active research field.

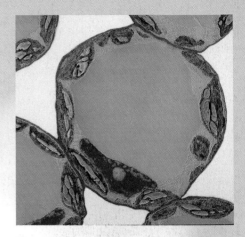

Figure 3 *Section through plant cell seen through an electron microscope. Note the cell wall (purple) around the cells, chloroplasts (green with pink starch grains) and permanent vacuole (blue). Magnification ×1000.*

Questions

1 What system of lenses gives a greater magnification than a simple hand lens? *[Total 1]*

2 Who was the first person to see the tiny blood vessels called capillaries? *[Total 1]*

3 What invention helped Robert Hooke describe cells? *[Total 1]*

4 State four different types of cell that Leeuwenhoek described in about 1670. *[Total 4]*

5 Who was the first person to describe a cell nucleus? *[Total 1]*

6 What is the 'cell theory' that Schlieden and Schwann suggested? *[Total 1]*

7 What type of microscope gave a better magnification than a light microscope. *[Total 1]*

8 What type of microscope gave three-dimensional pictures of the surfaces of small objects? *[Total 1]*

9 Draw a time-line for the development of microscopes. On it show when cells, named structures in cells and cell processes were discovered. *[Total 8]*

Applications

Insulation

Reindeer live in the Arctic where the temperature can be as low as −50 °C. They have a layer of fat under the skin to insulate them but this is used up as a source of energy and cannot be relied upon. Their fur coat must be very good at insulating them from the freezing temperatures. The hairs in the fur are adapted in two ways. First, the under-hair is very thick and traps a lot of air. Second, longer hairs are hollow so that more air is trapped and it makes the fur light and buoyant in water.

The advantages of hollow fibres were identified by scientists. They wanted to make a lightweight, waterproof and crush resistant fibre. In 1986 the first 'holofibre' called dacron was made from a polyester. The machinery to make the fine hollow fibre was difficult to build. Pillows, duvets, sleeping bags and furniture were filled with the new fibres. The design 'stolen' from the reindeer proved effective at keeping us warm.

Figure 1

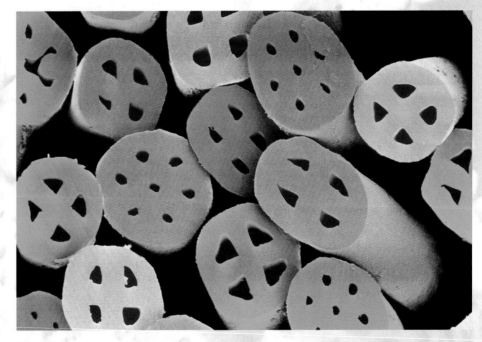

Figure 2 *Photomicrograph of a section across a dacron fibre. The holes trap air for lightness and insulation.*

Transplants

Sometimes organs fail in the body. Often the person will die unless medical help can be given. One type of help is to replace the organ. This is called transplant surgery. The first transplant of a heart was done by Professor Christiaan Barnard in 1967. After a transplant the patient can go on to have an active life.

A new organ must come from another living person or someone who has just died. This is a very sad time for the relatives and it is difficult for them to agree to the transplantation of the organ. There are not enough hearts or kidneys available for all the people who need them. Many patients die waiting for the chance to have the operation.

The problem with any transplant is that it may be rejected by the body and destroyed. To stop this drugs must be given. The drugs are used for all transplants but they make the patient more likely to catch infections.

If organs could be used from other animals instead of humans then there would be more available and give benefits to more patients. This is called xenotransplantation (see Section 7, chapter 5).

Figure 3 *These children have just finished the Transplant Games. The athletes in these Games have had organ transplants.*

Questions

1 Why do reindeer need hair? [Total 2]

2 How do the reindeer hairs provide insulation? [Total 2]

3 What is the main feature of dacron? [Total 1]

4 What is:
  a) an organ transplant [1]
  b) a xenotransplant? [1]
  [Total 2]

5 Why are transplants needed? [Total 2]

6 What is needed to stop the patient rejecting the transplant? [Total 1]

7 Why are xenotransplants necessary? [Total 1]

Questions

1 Plants and animals carry out life processes in slightly different ways. Under two columns, 'plants' and 'animals', write the relevant statements. Each could apply to only one or to both.

use energy   reproduce   move from place to place
grow   make their own food   take in water
respond quickly   *[Total 10]*

2 Copy and complete Table 1.   *[Total 7]*

Organ system	Organs or tissues	Specialised cell type
	lungs	lining cells (epithelial)
breathing system	trachea	
	blood	red blood cell
reproductive system	ovary	
transport system		root hair cell
nutritional system	leaf	
	stomach	muscle cell

Table 1

3 Explain the differences between an organism, an organ system, an organ, a tissue and a cell. *[Total 5]*

4 Draw labelled diagrams of a human cheek cell and a plant palisade cell. *[Total 10]*

5 Match up the statement with the cell type. Write out the statement and cell type. *[Total 10]*

Carries mucus and bacteria out of the lungs.	epithelial cell
Has a large store of food so it can divide and grow.	root hair cell
Is rectangular in shape and contains a large number of chloroplasts.	ciliated epithelium
Simple flattened cells on the surface of the skin.	white blood cell
Long and thin and can carry an electrical impulse.	bacterium
Is flexible and contains haemoglobin.	palisade cell
Carries water through a plant.	red blood cell
Can change shape to engulf a bacterium.	nerve cell
Does not contain a separate nucleus.	xylem vessel
Have a large surface area for absorption of minerals.	ovum cell

6 Figure 1 shows a fish and a seal. Suggest how the features labelled for each animal make it adapted for life in water. *[Total 8]*

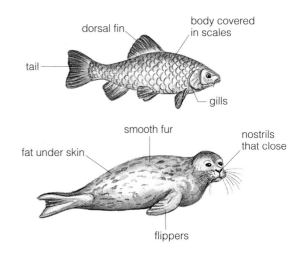

dorsal fin   body covered in scales
tail   gills
smooth fur   nostrils that close
fat under skin   flippers

Figure 1

7 Suggest reasons why a plant does not need a skeleton to support it but an animal does. *[Total 2]*

8 The amount of carbon dioxide in the air in a field of wheat changes during the day. The amount of water in the air was also recorded at the same time. The patterns are given in Figure 2.

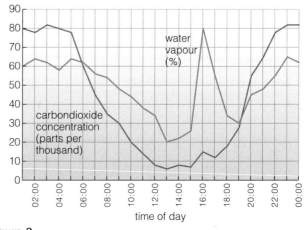

water vapour (%)

carbondioxide concentration (parts per thousand)

time of day

Figure 2

a) At what time of day does the amount of carbon dioxide start to decrease? [1]

b) What process speeds up at this time and why? [2]

c) What process returns the carbon dioxide to the air? [1]

d) Name two different groups of organisms that give out carbon dioxide. [2]

e) Suggest what may have caused the high water vapour level at 4 pm [1]

f) Describe how the pattern may be different in winter. [2]

[Total 9]

9 Tom tried to find out why different types of seaweed were found in different zones on the seashore. He said the zones depended on the time spent covered by sea water. He took some of the different seaweeds at four different zones, estimating the height above the low water mark.
He weighed the seaweeds then left them in the classroom in the same place for 24 hours and reweighed them. The results are given in Table 2.

Seaweed type	Height above low tide mark (m)	Initial mass (g)	Final mass (g)
A	1	100	60
A	3	120	73
B	3	120	84
C	5	100	80
D	5	120	106
D	8	80	72
E	8	80	78

Table 2

a) Find the difference in mass for each seaweed and height. What was the loss of mass due to? [8]

b) Which types of seaweed were sampled from two positions? [2]

c) Suggest a prediction that could be tested by sampling the same type of seaweed at different positions on the seashore. [2]

d) How could you make the loss of mass into a fair comparison between the types of seaweed? [1]

e) Plot a graph of average loss of mass against height above low water mark as a fair comparison. [8]

f) Describe the difference between the 'habitats' at the different heights above low water mark (the tidal range is 9 m). [3]

g) Suggest how the smaller loss of mass is an adaptation to the seaweed at the top of the shore. [2]

[Total 26]

10
R Find out what happens to organisms after they die.

11
R An *Amoeba* is a very small pond organism. Find out how it can carry out the seven life processes described in chapter 1.

12
R Find out how a type of animal or plant is able to live in its special habitat, e.g. how the blue whale breathes, feeds, moves, communicates, keeps warm and reproduces in the ocean.

13
R Find out about other materials that use holofibres. Why was it chosen for each purpose?

14
R Find out about the advances of xenotransplantation. Do you think it is right?

15
P What factors would affect the time of egg laying of blackbirds in a hedgerow?

16
P What factors would affect the growth of grass on the school playing field?

17
P How would you investigate the effect of wind on the distance a dandelion 'parachute' travels?

Food and Nutrition

2.1 Making food from sunlight

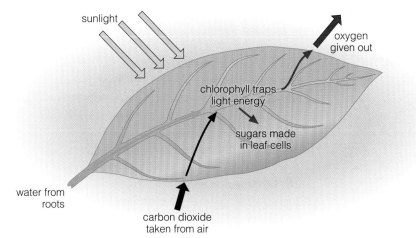

sunlight

oxygen
given out

chlorophyll traps
light energy

sugars made
in leaf cells

water from
roots

carbon dioxide
taken from air

Figure 1.1

How do plants make their own food? All they need are very simple substances and some energy. They use the substances produced to grow and to increase in mass.

Photosynthesis

The leaf is the organ where the plant makes food. The process is called **photosynthesis**. It uses light energy from the Sun to combine water with carbon dioxide (Figure 1.1). The products are oxygen and, glucose (a type of sugar). Glucose is used by the plant to make every other substance the plant needs.

The equation for photosynthesis is:

$$\text{water} + \text{carbon dioxide} \xrightarrow[\text{chlorophyll}]{\text{light energy}} \text{glucose} + \text{oxygen}$$

> !
>
> 1 square metre of sweetcorn plants take in about 2.2 kg of carbon dioxide to produce 0.55 kg of corn in a season. 1 square metre of rainforest absorbs about 54 000 kJ of energy each year but a young pine forest in the UK absorbs only 31 000 kJ each year.

Figure 1.2 *Evidence that light is needed for photosynthesis. The leaf on the left is attached to a plant in light. The leaf on the right has been tested for starch. The blue-black colour shows that starch has been produced only where light shone on the leaf.*

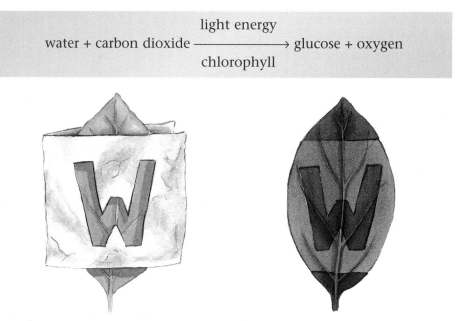

> !
>
> Plants only use about 1% of the sunlight reaching the surface of the Earth.

Light shines onto the large upper surface of each leaf and travels through the transparent upper layers until it is trapped by the **chlorophyll** in the chloroplasts of the palisade cells. The chloroplast uses the light energy from the Sun to split water molecules into oxygen and hydrogen. The chloroplast then combines the hydrogen with carbon dioxide to form **sugars**. The first sugar formed is **glucose**. The glucose is then turned into **starch** to be stored for a short time by the leaf cells.

A leaf needs raw materials to start the process of photosynthesis and must be able to get rid of the products. The structures in a leaf are arranged so that carbon dioxide and water flow into the leaf and glucose and oxygen can leave easily. (Figure 1.3).

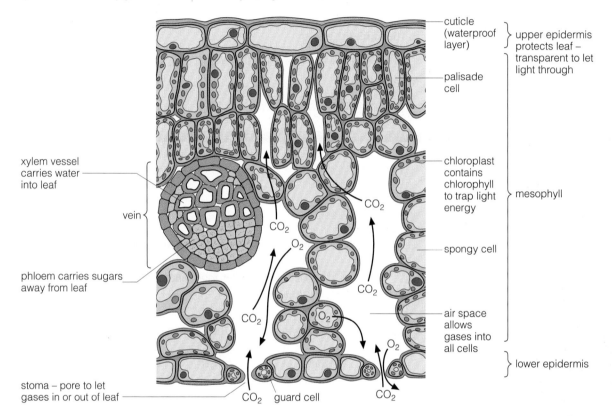

cuticle (waterproof layer)

upper epidermis protects leaf – transparent to let light through

palisade cell

xylem vessel carries water into leaf

vein

chloroplast contains chlorophyll to trap light energy

mesophyll

CO_2

CO_2

O_2

spongy cell

phloem carries sugars away from leaf

CO_2

air space allows gases into all cells

CO_2

O_2

lower epidermis

O_2

stoma – pore to let gases in or out of leaf

CO_2 guard cell

CO_2

Figure 1.3 *A section through a leaf.*

On a bright summer's day bubbles can be seen coming from pondweed. The bubbles are oxygen because the pondweed is photosynthesising quickly. On a dull day fewer bubbles are seen. This shows that the amount of light alters the rate of photosynthesis. In the laboratory, you can investigate this observation using bench lamps, pond water and pondweed.

Use of food

Glucose is used by the plant as a supply of energy. The glucose is made into sucrose to be carried away from the leaf. It can be stored as starch for later use or converted into other chemicals like cellulose for the cell walls. Some of the glucose is combined with minerals (for example, nitrates taken in by the roots) to make proteins needed for growth. Even the chlorophyll used in the process of photosynthesis must be made by the plant from glucose and minerals (in this case nitrogen and magnesium). Fats and oils found in seeds are also made from glucose.

> ! All of the oxygen in the atmosphere has come from photosynthesis. The atmosphere was changed by a group of organisms called the blue-green bacteria. They were the first to use chlorophyll and released oxygen from water. This happened between 3000 million and 1200 million years ago!

Summary

- Plants get their energy from sunlight.
- Photosynthesis needs chlorophyll to trap the sunlight energy.
- Photosynthesis combines water with carbon dioxide using sunlight energy.
- Glucose and oxygen are produced by photosynthesis.
- Glucose can be used to make starch, cellulose or other chemicals.

Questions

1 Copy and complete the following sentences. Plants make their own food using _____ energy, carbon dioxide from the air and _____ from the soil. The process is called _____. _____ (e.g. glucose) is produced and used to make all other substances the plant needs. _____ is a waste product. Leaves look _____ because they contain chlorophyll. The _____ traps the light energy. Most chlorophyll is in the _____ cells near the top surface of a leaf. *[Total 4]*

2 Give two functions of the roots of a plant. *[Total 2]*

3 List the raw materials and substances needed for photosynthesis. In a second column state where the plant gets the substance from. *[Total 8]*

4 List the first products from photosynthesis. In a second column state where the substance goes to when it moves out of the chloroplast. *[Total 4]*

5 Name five substances that plants make from the glucose produced in photosynthesis. *[Total 5]*

6 A shoot of pondweed was placed in a boiling tube of pond water. A bench lamp with a 60 W bulb shining on the tube was placed 20 cm away. An oxygen probe was put into the tube and the oxygen concentration recorded by a data-logger. The oxygen concentration was recorded after four minutes and again after a further five minutes. The experiment was repeated with the same pondweed but with the lamp 5 cm away from the boiling tube. The results are given in Table 1.1.

Distance of lamp (cm)	Oxygen concentration after 4 min (% saturation)	Oxygen concentration after 9 min (% saturation)
20	60	65
5	64	84

Table 1.1

a) Work out the increase in oxygen percentage per minute from the pondweed at 20 cm and 5 cm lamp distances. *[2]*

b) What is the effect of increasing the light on oxygen production. *[1]*

c) State the name of the process that produces the oxygen. *[1]*

d) Explain, in as much detail as you can, why the amount of oxygen produced in this experiment increased when the lamp was put closer to the pondweed. *[4]*

e) The lamp also gives off heat. Suggest how this could affect the results. *[2]*

[Total 10]

2.2 Gaining water and nutrients

Water is needed for life. How do animals and plants take in the water they need? Without enough water you feel thirsty and go for a drink. You swallow the water and it is absorbed into your blood from the digestive system. The water can then move to the tissues where it is needed and your thirst disappears.

A plant must stay still. The water is absorbed from the soil by the roots. Then it must move through the plant into the stem and leaves to get to all the cells needing the water. If the plant becomes short of water it wilts and may die.

Uptake of water

Water moves from the soil into the root hairs by **osmosis** (Figure 2.1). There is more water in the soil than in the root hair cells so the water moves through the selectively permeable cell membrane into the root hair cell.

> Osmosis is the movement of water from an area of high water concentration to an area of lower water concentration through a selectively permeable membrane.

The water will continue to move through the root cells, from cell to cell, until it reaches the **xylem vessels** in the middle of the root. It is then easy for the water to move through the hollow tubes of the xylem vessels, up the stem and into the veins of the leaf. The water moves to the leaf cells.

Water is used for photosynthesis, supporting the cells of the leaf or it evaporates into the air spaces and diffuses through the stomata into the air.

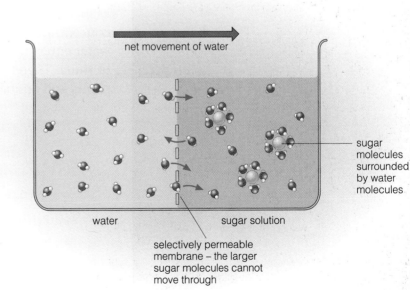

net movement of water

water

sugar solution

sugar molecules surrounded by water molecules

selectively permeable membrane – the larger sugar molecules cannot move through

Figure 2.1 *There is a higher concentration of water molecules on the left of the membrane. Water moves by osmosis from a higher concentration of water to a lower concentration of water. The larger sugar particles cannot move through the membrane.*

The evaporation of water into the air means that there is less water in the leaf cells and xylem vessels. Water moving up the stem replaces this lost water. The water is pulled up the plant using the force from evaporation of the water.

The movement of water through the plant is called the **transpiration stream**. (Figure 2.2).

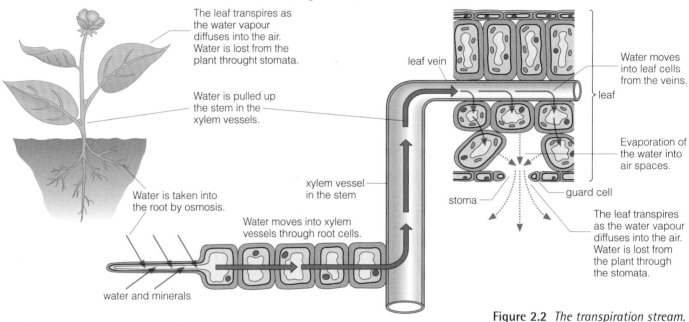

The leaf transpires as the water vapour diffuses into the air. Water is lost from the plant throught stomata.

Water is pulled up the stem in the xylem vessels.

Water is taken into the root by osmosis.

Water moves into xylem vessels through root cells.

water and minerals

leaf vein

xylem vessel in the stem

stoma

Water moves into leaf cells from the veins.

leaf

Evaporation of the water into air spaces.

guard cell

The leaf transpires as the water vapour diffuses into the air. Water is lost from the plant through the stomata.

Figure 2.2 *The transpiration stream.*

Absorption of water into animal cells or into the blood also occurs by osmosis. The water moves from where there is a higher water concentration to where there is a lower water concentration e.g. from the intestines into the blood. The water enters the cytoplasm of the body cells that are short of water. Therefore the water is absorbed in the same way by plants and animals – by osmosis.

Figure 2.3 *The transpiration stream can even transport water to the top of a giant sequoia tree.*

What is water needed for?

Your body is about 70% water. If you weigh 50 kg then there is about 35 litres of water in the body. About 2.5 litres are found in the blood, so most is surrounding the cells as tissue fluid or in the cytoplasm of cells. The water is used in the following ways:

- As a solvent, to let all the other chemicals dissolve. The chemicals can then be carried in the water or move about by random motion of the molecules.
- As part of a chemical reaction. Water is often one of the reactants e.g. the breakdown of food in the intestine or in photosynthesis.
- As a coolant. The water forms part of sweat released onto the skin and is evaporated, so it takes away the heat with the vapour. Water also evaporates from plant leaves when the sun shines on the leaf. The evaporation stops the leaf getting too hot. Most of the water absorbed by a plant is lost in this way. The loss of water is called transpiration.
- For support. Water, like other liquids, cannot be squashed into a smaller space. Plants fill up their cells so that there is a push against the cell wall. The cells become firm and cannot be squashed. The plant weight is then supported by these stiff cells. Some animals also use a similar system in their whole body to keep their shape, e.g. an earthworm.

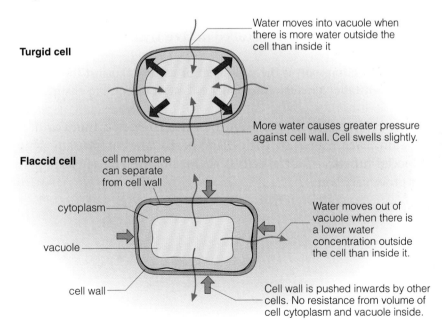

Turgid cell

Water moves into vacuole when there is more water outside the cell than inside it

More water causes greater pressure against cell wall. Cell swells slightly.

Flaccid cell

cell membrane can separate from cell wall

cytoplasm

vacuole

cell wall

Water moves out of vacuole when there is a lower water concentration outside the cell than inside it.

Cell wall is pushed inwards by other cells. No resistance from volume of cell cytoplasm and vacuole inside.

Figure 2.4 *Turgid and flaccid cells.*

> **!** If a red blood cell is put into water it will burst. The membrane is too weak to hold the cell together when it takes in the water.

Uptake of nutrients

Water moves into both plants and animals by osmosis. Do nutrients enter both types of organism in the same way?

The nutrients for a plant must come from the soil and are absorbed along with the water. They are called mineral salts. The plant needs them in small or minute amounts compared to the amount of carbon dioxide and water used in photosynthesis. Animals also need the same mineral salts which must come from their food.

A mineral salt is soluble in water and the mineral particles can move about. They will always move from where there are more of them to where there are less. The concentration will eventually become equal in all places. This movement is called **diffusion**.

> Diffusion is the movement of particles from an area of high concentration to an area of lower concentration due to the random motion of the particles.

If a mineral salt is in a higher concentration in the soil than in the root then the mineral can diffuse into the root hair and so into the plant. However, many of the minerals are in short supply in the soil. The root hair cells use energy to absorb the mineral salt particles from the soil into the root. The selective cell membrane makes sure that the mineral cannot leave the cell to return to the soil. The process of using energy to absorb a substance is called **active transport**.

> Active transport is the movement of particles against the concentration gradient, through a cell membrane, using energy.

Plants need mineral salts like nitrates, phosphates, potassium and magnesium. Each is used by the cells to make new compounds which have special functions in the cell. Without the mineral salts the plants do not grow very well.

> **!** Plant roots must be fussy. Some minerals are poisonous. Too much copper, lead or aluminium can kill a plant so these minerals must be kept out.

Mineral salt	Compound in plant	Use in the plant
nitrate	proteins	growth of new cells
phosphate	ATP	chemical energy in cells
potassium	enzyme activators	helps reactions of photosynthesis
magnesium	chlorophyll	trap light in photosynthesis

Table 2.1 *Uses of mineral salts in plants.*

Animals also need mineral salts. They absorb them through the intestine. The lining of the intestine behaves like a selectively permeable membrane. The mineral salts can diffuse or be actively transported into the blood in just the same way as into the plant root.

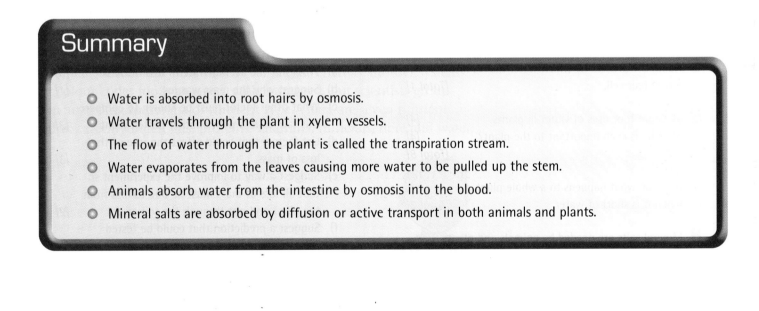

Summary

- Water is absorbed into root hairs by osmosis.
- Water travels through the plant in xylem vessels.
- The flow of water through the plant is called the transpiration stream.
- Water evaporates from the leaves causing more water to be pulled up the stem.
- Animals absorb water from the intestine by osmosis into the blood.
- Mineral salts are absorbed by diffusion or active transport in both animals and plants.

Carbohydrates

Carbohydrates contain the elements carbon, hydrogen and oxygen. There is always twice as much hydrogen as there is oxygen (e.g. glucose $C_6H_{12}O_6$). Carbohydrates are used for energy storage or release of energy in cells.

There are two sub-groups of carbohydrates.

- Simple carbohydrates (sugars) are sweet and dissolve easily. An example of a useful sugar in humans is **glucose**. The glucose is broken down in cells to release energy during respiration.
- Complex carbohydrates (polysaccharides) are large molecules made of many glucose units. They are not sweet and are used to store energy. Humans store energy as a chemical called glycogen. The common carbohydrate stored in plants is starch which is in foods like potatoes and bread.

All carbohydrates can be broken down in respiration to release about 17 kJ/g.

Nutrient group	Good sources	Uses
carbohydrates		
○ sugars	sweets, cakes	provide instant energy
○ polysaccharides	bread, rice, cereals, pasta, potatoes	instant energy or energy storage (glycogen in humans)
fats	butter, cooking oil, cream, red meat	energy storage making cell membranes
proteins	meat, eggs, fish, nuts, peas	growth and repair (making new cells)
mineral salts		
○ calcium	milk	bones and teeth
○ iron	red meat	red blood cells
○ sodium	salt and processed foods	water balance in cells
vitamins		
○ A	fish oils, butter	aids night vision
○ B	liver, cereals, meat	chemical reactions in respiration
○ C	fresh fruit and vegetables	healthy skin and gums
○ D	dairy products, fatty fish	absorption and use of calcium for bones and teeth
fibre	cereals, vegetables, fruit	keeps food flowing smoothly in digestive system
water	drinks, soggy foods	dissolves chemicals in cells or tissue fluids.

Table 3.1 *Nutrients, sources and uses of foods.*

Fats

These also contain carbon, hydrogen and oxygen but there is very little oxygen compared to the amount of hydrogen (e.g. tristearin fat found in beef has the formula $C_{51}H_{104}O_6$). **Fats** do not dissolve in water and so have to be carried in the blood in a special way. They are combined with proteins (Figure 3.3). When broken down in respiration, fats give out twice as much energy as carbohydrates (34 kJ/g). Fats are made from two different parts – fatty acids and glycerol.

Fats can be taken into cells and broken down in respiration if energy is needed straight away or they can be stored in special cells under the skin. The fats form a concentrated energy store for the long term.

Protein

Proteins are large molecules made up from chains of **amino acids**. Each amino acid contains the elements carbon, hydrogen, oxygen and nitrogen. Some amino acids also contain sulphur. Most amino acids can be made by our cells but some must be in our food. The amino acids which cannot be made by our bodies are called **essential amino acids**. Animal products like meat have more essential amino acids than plant products such as beans.

The protein in food is used by cells for growth and repair. This means that structures in new cells are made of proteins and the ability to carry out chemical reactions in the cells depends upon other proteins (enzymes).

Proteins can also be used for energy if the body is starving and no carbohydrate or fat is available. They are broken down into carbon dioxide, water and urea.

The chemical tests for the major nutrients in food are given in Table 3.2. In each test a small sample of food is ground up with a little water and put in a test tube. Several procedures are carried out. Eye protection must be worn.

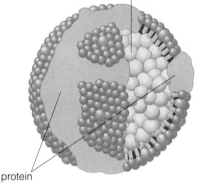

fat molecules in centre of globule protected by the protein

protein

Figure 3.3 *Fat combined with protein carried in the blood.*

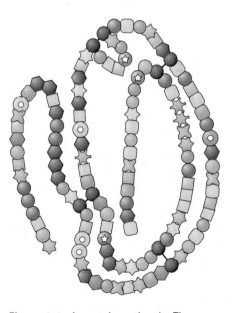

Figure 3.4 *A protein molecule. The different shapes represent the amino acids. A protein can be made from between 50 and 3000 amino acids joined in a long chain and folded up.*

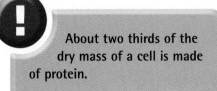

About two thirds of the dry mass of a cell is made of protein.

Nutrient	Test name	Method	Result	Before	After
Sugar (except sucrose)	Benedicts' test	○ Dissolve food in 1 cm³ water. ○ Add 2 cm³ Benedicts' solution. ○ Boil using a water bath for 1 minute.	Blue solution becomes red.		
Starch	Iodine test	○ Add several drops of iodine solution.	Straw colour turns to blue-black.		
Fat	Emulsion test	○ Cut food into thin shavings without any water. ○ Add 5 cm³ of ethanol. ○ Shake well then leave to settle. ○ Half fill a second test tube with water. ○ Carefully add drops of the solution from the first test tube to the water.	Water becomes cloudy	Dropping pipette Ethanol Food sample / Water	Ethanol / Cloudy / Water
Protein	Biuret test	○ Add 1 cm³ of dilute sodium hydroxide. ○ Add 3 drops of 1% copper sulphate solution. ○ Shake and watch	Pale blue colour turns to violet.	Drops of copper sulpahte solution Sodium hydroxide	

Table 3.2 *Chemical tests for the major nutrients in food.*

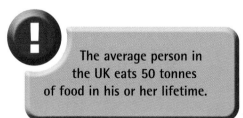

The average person in the UK eats 50 tonnes of food in his or her lifetime.

Mineral salts

These soluble chemicals are the same as the nutrients needed by plants. Many foods contain different amounts of them but we usually need small amounts compared to the three major nutrient groups already described (see Table 3.1).

Calcium is needed for the structure of bones and teeth, iron for carrying oxygen in red blood cells, and sodium for keeping the correct concentration of substances in the cells by allowing water to move into or out of the cell. In addition, phosphorus is needed for energy release and potassium to help the chemical reactions in cells (respiration).

A deficiency of a mineral in the diet causes specific symptoms (signs) called a **deficiency disease** e.g. lack of iron causes anaemia, lack of calcium causes rickets. Too much of a mineral can also cause health problems.

Vitamins

The majority of this group of chemicals cannot be made in the body- they must be eaten in our food. Without enough of each vitamin, deficiency diseases occur eg. lack of vitamin C causes scurvy. Each vitamin has a special job to do in the body. Some of the vitamins and their jobs are described in Table 3.1. The vitamins have been given letters but each does have a special name, e.g. vitamin C is called ascorbic acid. None of the vitamins provides energy.

Fibre

This is not a special chemical but a group of substances that the body cannot digest. **Fibre** in the digestive system helps the movement of all the other substances along the canal. The fibre encourages the right types of bacteria to grow in the large intestine so that fewer poisons are produced from harmful bacteria. The waste food can be removed from the body easily because fibre provides the bigger bulk.

A large amount of fibre comes from plant cell walls. The cell walls contain cellulose that humans cannot break down. Therefore, plant matter is very important in a balanced diet to prevent diarrhoea or constipation and cancer of the colon.

Water

About 70% of your body mass is water.
The water is important for four reasons.

- Water dissolves most of the other chemicals in the body and allows the chemical reactions to go ahead.
- The water transports the substances around the body.
- Some reactions need water as a raw material. It is a substrate for the reaction.
- Water is used to cool the body. It is lost by evaporation from sweat.

Water is lost from the body when you breathe out, through urine, faeces and through sweat. The diet must have sufficient water in it to make up for the loss.

! Only humans, chimpanzees, fruit bats and guinea pigs cannot make vitamin C and need it in their diet.

Figure 3.5

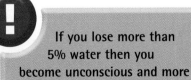

! If you lose more than 5% water then you become unconscious and more than 8% loss causes death.

Balanced diets

A **balanced diet** has all of the nutrients required by the body to keep it healthy and in the correct amounts. Any diet that causes any health problem causes malnourishment.

People who take in too much energy, by eating either too much carbohydrate or fat, will become obese. The extra weight carried by the body means the heart must pump blood to more tissues. The extra pumping puts a strain on the heart. Obese people are more likely to have a heart attack. In Britain in 1998, it was estimated that over 60% of adults and 50% of fifteen year olds were overweight. (Overweight is defined as 15% greater than the ideal mass for the height and build).

Too little food causes tiredness and wasting diseases which are most common in developing countries.

Eating most of the carbohydrate you need as sugar is bad for your teeth. Bacteria in your mouth use the sugar and produce acids. The acids rot the teeth. It is best to have a little sugar with meals instead of continuously eating sweets during the day.

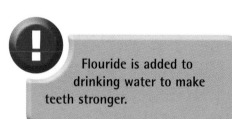

Flouride is added to drinking water to make teeth stronger.

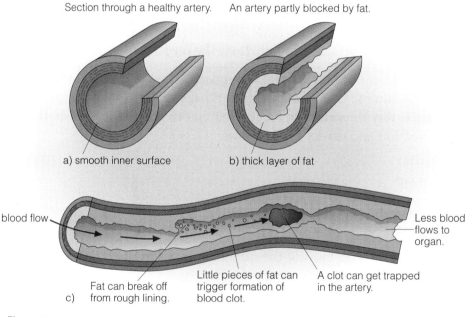

Section through a healthy artery.   An artery partly blocked by fat.

a) smooth inner surface   b) thick layer of fat

blood flow   Less blood flows to organ.

c)   Fat can break off from rough lining.   Little pieces of fat can trigger formation of blood clot.   A clot can get trapped in the artery.

Figure 3.6

Fish and plant oils are more easily carried in the blood than animals fats.

If there is too much fat in the diet some is left in the blood vessels as it travels round. This narrows the vessels and causes a strain on the heart. The fatty deposit can trigger the formation of blood clots which can block narrow blood vessels. If a blood clot gets stuck in the brain, it causes a stroke. If it gets stuck in the blood vessels feeding the heart muscle with oxygen then a heart attack can occur.

Too much salt in food makes it more difficult for the heart to pump the blood. The blood pressure rises. This means that the heart cannot respond sufficiently when you exercise. You get tired more quickly.

It is recommended that you should eat less processed foods e.g. sausages, beefburgers, crisps because they contain too much fat and salt. In food processing, most of the fibre is removed even from vegetables. Fresh fruit, pasta, wholemeal bread and white meats are recommended for supplying a balanced diet. Five servings of fruit or vegetables are recommended every day.

Summary

- Carbohydrates, e.g. starch and sugar, give us energy.
- Fats give twice as much energy as carbohydrates.
- Fats and carbohydrates can be stored in the body.
- Too much fat in the diet leads to heart disease.
- Too much energy rich food makes us overweight and this can also cause heart disease.
- Proteins are used for growth and repair of cells. They cannot be stored.
- Vitamins and minerals are needed to help special chemical reactions in the body.
- A balanced diet contains all the nutrients in the amounts needed by the body.
- Fibre helps the muscle contractions that move food through the gut.

Questions

1 Copy and complete the following sentences.
Food is made up of many chemical _____.
A _____ diet contains all of the substances needed by the body in the correct amounts.
_____ give the body energy when they are broken down. Fats give twice as much energy as _____. Proteins are needed for _____ and repair of tissues. _____ like calcium are needed for special functions in the body. Calcium helps to make _____ or teeth strong and hard. Most _____ cannot be made in the body. If the body is short of a vitamin
a _____ disease occurs, e.g. scurvy is a lack of vitamin C. Fibre is important to help the food move along the gut and to stop _____ of the colon. *[Total 5]*

2 Group the foods in the list below in five different ways, according to the following categories. Each food should only be put into one group for each exercise. Rice, bread, potatoes, chips, pasta, cereal, milk, eggs, cheese, butter, museli, chocolate, crisps, chicken, bacon, sausages, cooking oil, bananas, oranges, carrots, baked beans, ice cream.
a) Department of Health groups (breads; fruit and vegetables; meat and fish; dairy products; manufactured foods with high salt or fat). *[2]*
b) Groups found on a supermarket shelf. *[2]*
c) Healthy (green), satisfactory (amber) and unhealthy (red). *[2]*
[Total 6]

3 a) How are fats carried in the human body? *[1]*
b) Why is this necessary? *[1]*
[Total 2]

4 Explain why all diets must contain some protein.
[Total 2]

5 What is the difference between an essential and non-essential amino acid? *[Total 2]*

6 Name types of food that contain:
a) essential amino acids *[1]*
b) non-essential amino acids. *[1]*
[Total 2]

7 Where does fibre come from in our diet? *[Total 1]*

8 What is water used for in the body? *[Total 4]*

9 A beefburger contains 40 g of fat and 70 g of carbohydrate. How much more energy does the fat provide than the carbohydrate? *[Total 3]*

10 Describe how you carry out a chemical test for sugars in some sweets. Explain what you would see. *[Total 4]*

11 Megan wanted to find the energy content of some snack foods. She accurately weighed the snack food, placed it on a mounted needle, lit it and quickly held it under a boiling tube of water. The temperature increase of the water was recorded (Figure 3.7)

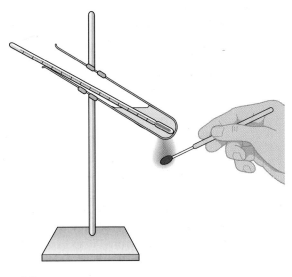

Figure 3.7

a) List the measurements needed for the experiment [4]

b) The temperature increase worked out at an energy value for 100 g of 957 kJ. The packet information said it was 2257 kJ/100 g. Suggest four different reasons why her value was much less than the value on the packet. [4]

c) Suggest ways that the apparatus or method could be changed, still using school laboratory equipment, to improve the accuracy of the results. [3]

d) List the factors that must be kept the same to compare the energy content of several different snack foods. [4]

[Total 15]

2.4 Digestion in humans

How does the human body take in food and use it to grow? Food for humans comes from plants or other animals. The food is made from large molecules which cannot be absorbed into the blood. They must be broken down, absorbed and then changed into the form needed by our own bodies.

The digestive system

The organ system that has the job of taking in food and making it available for the rest of the body is the **digestive system**. It is a long tube running through the body from the mouth to the anus. Special chemicals called **enzymes** are released to break down the food. This process is called **digestion**. The digested food is then absorbed into the blood stream. Any food that cannot be digested is passed out of the anus, by a process called **egestion**.

The digestive system consists of many organs, each specialised for one function. The food passes through the organs in sequence so that it can be progressively broken down and then absorbed.

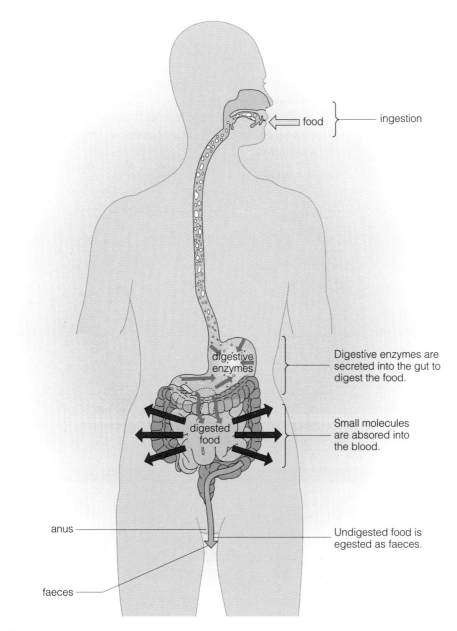

food — ingestion

Digestive enzymes are secreted into the gut to digest the food.

digestive enzymes

digested food

Small molecules are absored into the blood.

anus

Undigested food is egested as faeces.

faeces

Figure 4.1 *Processes in the digestive system*

The mouth and ingestion

Ingestion is the act of taking food into the mouth. It is chewed to break it down into smaller pieces and to mix it with saliva. The smaller pieces are easier to swallow and have a bigger surface area for enzymes to break down the food.

The **saliva** contains mucus which helps to lubricate the food. It also contains an enzyme which breaks down starch into simple sugar molecules (Figure 4.2).

Enzymes are special chemicals that speed up chemical reactions. They are made of protein and each enzyme has a very specific shape. This special shape means that a substrate molecule can fit into the enzyme and be broken down in digestion. Anything that changes the shape of the enzyme will mean that it does not work any more. Enzymes are used for many chemical reactions in the body. They are useful in digestion because they help to break down the food. The enzyme in your saliva is called amylase and it starts work on digesting your food in your mouth.

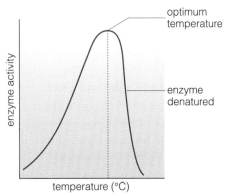

Figure 4.3 *Enzymes change shape if they are heated. This is called denaturing. The substrate molecule does not fit the active site any more.*

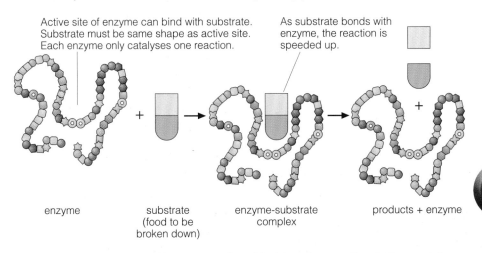

Active site of enzyme can bind with substrate. Substrate must be same shape as active site. Each enzyme only catalyses one reaction.

As substrate bonds with enzyme, the reaction is speeded up.

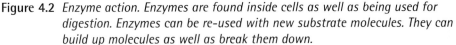

enzyme

substrate (food to be broken down)

enzyme-substrate complex

products + enzyme

Figure 4.2 *Enzyme action. Enzymes are found inside cells as well as being used for digestion. Enzymes can be re-used with new substrate molecules. They can build up molecules as well as break them down.*

Teeth are also important for digestion in the mouth. They are special structures which have a very hard coating on the surface. They grow from the jaw bones. Each type of tooth is adapted to its function in the mouth. The incisors at the front have a sharp edge for biting and the molars at the back have a broad surface with cusps to crush the food into small pieces.

The jaw muscles of a shark can exert a force of 600 N between the teeth – creating the greatest pressure (30 000 N/cm²) in the body.

Figure 4.4

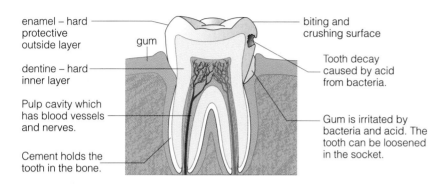

enamel – hard protective outside layer

gum

dentine – hard inner layer

Pulp cavity which has blood vessels and nerves.

Cement holds the tooth in the bone.

biting and crushing surface

Tooth decay caused by acid from bacteria.

Gum is irritated by bacteria and acid. The tooth can be loosened in the socket.

Figure 4.5 *Section through a molar tooth.*

> Elephants have seven sets of teeth. Once the final set of teeth has worn out they die because they cannot chew vegetation any more.

Humans have two sets of teeth. When young, the jaw grows but the teeth cannot. The second set is larger than the first and there are 12 more teeth in total. If you look after your teeth, this makes sure you can chew your food for all of your life. The structure of a tooth can be seen in Figure 4.5.

The food is swallowed by a special action that covers the windpipe when the food is pushed down the **oesophagus** by the tongue. If food 'goes down the wrong way' i.e. goes towards the lungs, we cough to force the food back up.

The food travels down the oesophagus by **peristalsis** (Figure 4.6).

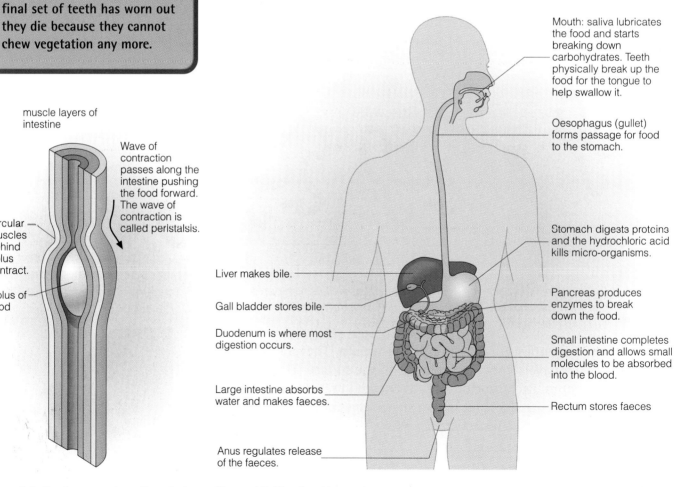

muscle layers of intestine

Wave of contraction passes along the intestine pushing the food forward. The wave of contraction is called peristalsis.

Circular muscles behind bolus contract.

bolus of food

Mouth: saliva lubricates the food and starts breaking down carbohydrates. Teeth physically break up the food for the tongue to help swallow it.

Oesophagus (gullet) forms passage for food to the stomach.

Stomach digests proteins and the hydrochloric acid kills micro-organisms.

Pancreas produces enzymes to break down the food.

Liver makes bile.

Gall bladder stores bile.

Duodenum is where most digestion occurs.

Small intestine completes digestion and allows small molecules to be absorbed into the blood.

Large intestine absorbs water and makes faeces.

Rectum stores faeces

Anus regulates release of the faeces.

Figure 4.6 *Food moves along the whole of the intestine by peristalsis.*

Figure 4.7 *The digestive system.*

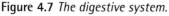

Digestion in the stomach and intestines

Food that has been swallowed enters the **stomach**. The stomach expands with the food eaten. Rings of muscle at the stomach entrance and exit control the direction and rate of flow of the food. A meal containing fat and protein remains longer in the stomach than a meal with only carbohydrates. The average time for food to stay in the stomach is about four hours.

The stomach walls are in constant motion. The churning of the stomach helps to physically break up the food and to mix it with the **gastric juice** produced by glands in the walls. The juice is mainly hydrochloric acid which kills most micro-organisms in the food. An enzyme breaks down proteins into smaller molecules.

The acid mush is released from the stomach into the small intestine in small amounts. It is neutralised by alkaline secretions from the liver (bile) and **pancreas**. In the small intestine many different enzymes are used to break down the large molecules in foods (see Table 4.1). **Proteases** digest proteins, **lipases** break down fats and **carbohydrases** digest carbohydrates. **Bile** contains substances that make the fats form tiny droplets in water. The fats can then be broken down more easily.

> **!** Stress often causes too much acid to be made by the stomach. If any part of the stomach is inflamed then the acid and resistant bacteria further irritate the stomach lining. An ulcer is formed which can be very painful.

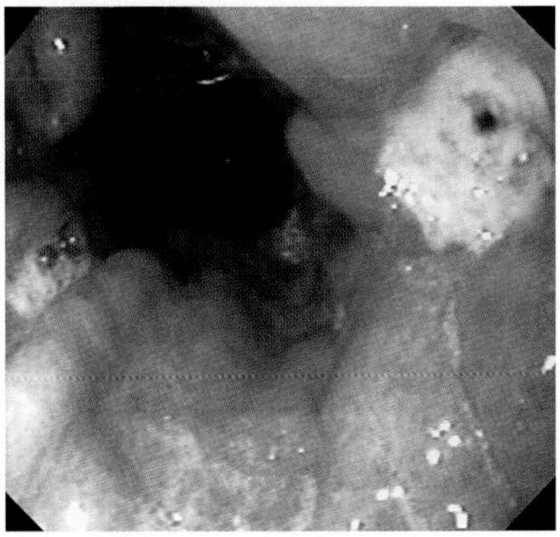

Figure 4.8 *An ulcer in the stomach.*

Area of alimentary canal	Enzyme	Gland producing enzyme	Food broken down	Products formed
mouth	amylase (carbohydrase)	salivary gland	starch	maltose
stomach	protease	gastric gland	protein	polypeptides
small intestine	amylase (carbohydrase)	pancreas	starch	maltose
small intestine	lipase	pancreas	fats	fatty acids and glycerol
small intestine	protease	pancreas and wall of small intestine	proteins and polypeptides	amino acids
small intestine	carbohydrases	wall of small intestine	milk and fruit sugars	simplest sugars, e.g. glucose

Table 4.1 *Digestion of foods by enzymes.*

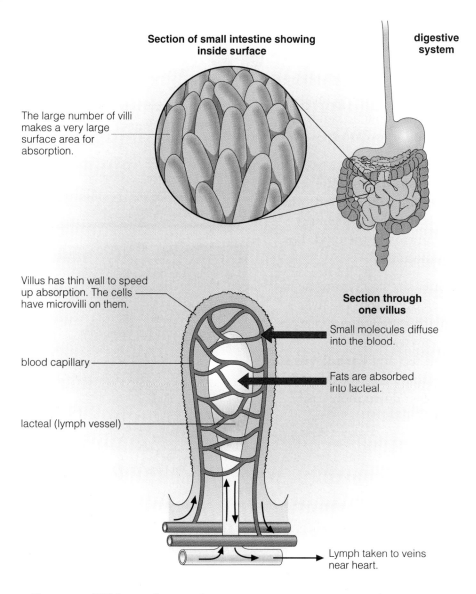

Section of small intestine showing inside surface

digestive system

The large number of villi makes a very large surface area for absorption.

Villus has thin wall to speed up absorption. The cells have microvilli on them.

Section through one villus

Small molecules diffuse into the blood.

Fats are absorbed into lacteal.

blood capillary

lacteal (lymph vessel)

Lymph taken to veins near heart.

Figure 4.9 *Villi have a large surface area for absorption of digested food.*

Absorption in the small intestine

The small intestine has a massive surface area (about $300\,m^2$) for absorption of the digested food molecules. The surface area is increased by the following:

- It is long (approximately 7 m)
- The absorbing surface (inside the tube) is folded so there is a larger surface
- On the folds are villi which stick up from the surface like many fingers.
- Each villus has tiny projections called microvilli.

The soluble food is absorbed into the blood by diffusion. However, if some substances are in short supply, the lining cells of the villi can use energy to help absorb them quickly. The blood goes to the liver and any poisons that have been absorbed with the digested food can be destroyed.

The large intestine

This is the area where most water is absorbed into the blood. Some of the bacteria in the large intestine can use the remains of the food to make some vitamins the body needs. These are absorbed with the water. The remainder of the undigested food needs the fibre to help it move smoothly through the large intestine.

The faeces are stored in the last part of the large intestine and must be removed from the body regularly. This process is called egestion.

Egestion means getting rid of undigested food that has not been absorbed into the cells of the body. Egestion should not be confused with excretion which means getting rid of waste substances from within the cells of the body e.g carbon dioxide and urea.

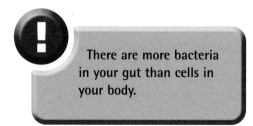

There are more bacteria in your gut than cells in your body.

Summary

- Digestion breaks down large food substances into small, soluble molecules for absorption into the blood.
- Enzymes speed up chemical reactions including the breakdown of substances.
- Enzymes are specific for each reaction. Carbohydrases break down carbohydrates, proteases break down protein and lipases break down fats.
- The small intestine completes digestion and absorbs the soluble molecules.
- The food moves along the digestive system by peristalsis.

Questions

1 Copy and complete the following sentences.
Food must be made soluble for it to be
_____ into the blood. It is broken down
by _____ into simple chemicals. Each
_____ has an active site which is a special
shape for the reacting chemical.
The stomach is acidic to _____ micro-
organisms in the food. The acid is _____ by
pancreatic juice and bile in the small intestine. The bile
breaks up fats into tiny droplets for the _____
enzyme to digest. The digested food is _____
into the blood in the small intestine. Undigested
food is _____. *[Total 4]*

2 Name the four processes that occur along
the length of the alimentary canal. *[Total 4]*

3 Describe how food is pushed through
the alimentary canal. *[Total 3]*

4 Give three ways that the surface area
of the small intestine is increased. *[Total 3]*

5 2 cm² of boiled egg white (containing undigested
protein) is put into a series of test tubes labelled A,
B, C and D. Substances are added to the tubes as
shown in Table 4.2. The tubes were placed in a beaker
of warm water (37 °C) and the time required for the
liquid to become clear was recorded.

Tube	A	B	C	D
Substances added	1 cm³ water, 1 cm³ protease	1 cm³ acid, 1 cm³ water	1 cm³ acid, 1 cm³ protease	1 cm³ acid, 1 cm³ boiled protease
Time for solution to be clear (min)	15	still cloudy after 30 min	2	20

Table 4.2

a) List the reactions in order, fastest first. *[1]*
b) Suggest why the solutions became clear. *[2]*
c) What was the effect of the acid on the speed of the reaction? *[1]*
d) State the tubes you compared to give your answer to part c). Explain your reason. *[2]*
e) Suggest why boiling the protease slowed down the reaction. *[2]*
f) What is the purpose of tube B in the experiment? *[2]*
[Total 10]

History

Why are the English called limeys?

The thought that a disease could be caused by something missing from the diet must have occurred to many people. The ancient Greek physician Hippocrates recommended eating 'raw liver' as a cure for night-blindness. Folklore (or traditional remedies) used many different foods for curing illnesses.

The captain's log from Ferdinand Magellan's voyage around the world (1519–1522) gave detailed descriptions of scurvy in the crew and officers.

> '... we sailed the space of three months and 20 days, without tasting any fresh provisions. The biscuit we were eating. ... it was nothing but dust, and worms which had consumed the substance; ... we were obliged to subsist on saw-dust, and even mice were sought after with such avidity that they sold for half a ducat a piece.
>
> Nor was this all, our greatest misfortune was being attacked by a malady in which the gums swelled so as to hide the teeth, as well in the upper as the lower jaw, whence those affected thus were incapable of chewing their food.'

As the disease got worse the men became very tired and could not do any work. Many ships were wrecked because the crew were too tired to sail. Some captains thought that the sailors were simply lazy.

Sir Richard Hawkins found that oranges and lemons were 'a certain remedie for this infirmite' on his expedition around the world which began in 1593. Other sailors also purchased lemons before long journeys but they were difficult to keep fresh.

James Lind, a British naval doctor, carried out a careful scientific study in 1747 to find the cure for scurvy. He found that the only treatment which prevented scurvy was to eat oranges and lemons. In 1753, he published *A treatise on the scurvy*. It described that within a week of eating two oranges and one lemon each day, signs of scurvy disappeared from the sailors. Captain Cook put this knowledge to good effect in his voyages around the world in the 1770s. Captain Cook introduced raisins and sauerkraut as well as citrus fruits and he never missed an opportunity to take on board fresh fruit and vegetables.

In 1795, lemon juice was made compulsory for Royal Navy crews. Sixty years later the merchant seamen were required to take lemon juice. The sailors became called 'limeys' because when they docked in America, the Americans thought they were drinking lime juice after the long sea passage. However, lime juice is not as effective as lemon juice in preventing scurvy.

Figure 1 *James Lind.*

Despite this evidence nobody knew what was in the fruit that prevented the disease. The cure was associated with sharp tastes (acids) and many were tried – even sulphuric acid! It was not until 1928 that the active ingredient of the fruit juice was found. It was first manufactured in 1933 and it is called vitamin C (ascorbic acid). The RDA (recommended daily amount) is 0.04 g, a tiny amount compared to carbohydrates but enough to help form the chemicals needed in the cells of the skin, blood vessels and bones.

Figure 2 *A sailor being treated for scurvy.*

Questions

1 What is the chemical name for vitamin C?   *[Total 1]*

2 a) Name the person who recommended eating fresh fruit to stop scurvy following an experiment with six different diets.   *[1]*
b) What was his job in the navy?   *[1]*
   [Total 2]

3 a) Why do you think that sailors often suffered from malnutrition?   *[2]*
b) What are the signs of scurvy?   *[3]*
   [Total 5]

4 a) What is meant by the RDA?   *[1]*
b) What is the RDA for vitamin C?   *[1]*
   [Total 2]

5 What did Captain Cook do to stop his sailors getting scurvy on his voyages?   *[Total 2]*

6 a) Who called the English sailors 'Limeys'?   *[1]*
b) Why were they given this name?   *[1]*
   [Total 2]

Applications

Food in space

Figure 1 *Space food.*

Eating in micro-gravity conditions in space does not change what you need to eat. But it *does* affect the packaging and the form of the food.

The mass of the food to be put into orbit must be kept to a minimum. The mass allowed for food is limited to 1.7 kg per person per day, which includes 454 g of packaging for each person each day. If possible, foods are dehydrated and water is added in the spacecraft. The space shuttle fuel cells, which produce electricity by combining hydrogen and oxygen, provide ample water for rehydrating foods as well as drinking.

Diets are designed to supply each crew member with all the recommended dietary allowances (RDA) of vitamins and minerals necessary to perform in the environment of space. Energy requirements are determined by the US National Research Council formula for basal energy expenditure (BEE). Astronauts may even design their own menus but these must be checked by a dietitian to ensure they consume a balanced supply of nutrients.

Foods are analysed for use on the space shuttle through nutritional analysis, sensory evaluation, freeze drying, rehydration, storage studies, packaging evaluations, and many other methods. However, before any food is used on the space shuttle, it must be tested by people on the NASA zero-gravity KC-135 aeroplane, affectionately known as the 'vomit comet'. Their job is to see how the food item will react in micro-gravity. A food item is added to the menu only after it has undergone all the necessary research and development, and is approved for flight.

Food is packaged and stowed in the locker trays in Houston about a month before each launch. Stowed food lockers and shipping containers are kept refrigerated. About three weeks before launch, the food lockers are shipped to Kennedy Space Center (KSC) in Florida. There they are refrigerated until they are installed in the space shuttle 2–3 days before launch. Besides the meal and pantry food lockers, a fresh food locker is packed at KSC and installed on the space shuttle 18–24 hours before launch. The fresh food locker contains tortillas, fresh bread, breakfast rolls, and fresh fruits and vegetables such as apples, bananas, oranges, carrot and celery sticks. The carrots and celery must be used within 2 days.

Uses of enzymes

Enzymes are big business. They are used in many industrial processes as well as in the home as 'biological washing powders'. Some of the advantages of using enzymes are:

- They speed up reactions so processing is quicker.
- They allow reactions at lower temperatures and lower pressures than would be needed without them. Therefore the process is cheaper and easier to control.
- They are very precise so that special reactions can take place without affecting other substances in the process.

Some people are ill when they drink normal milk because they do not have the right enzyme to digest it. The milk sugar (lactose) must be removed so that allergic people can benefit from the protein and minerals that are in the milk.

The enzyme which breaks down the milk sugar is taken from bacteria. The enzyme is trapped (immobilised) inside porous capsules and put into a long column. Pasteurised milk is passed through the column and the milk sugar is broken down. The modified milk is packaged and sold in shops as lactose-free milk.

Another use of enzymes is to produce the soft centres of chocolates. Inside the hard chocolate casing a thick paste of starch and relevant flavours is introduced. The enzymes amylase and maltase are added in minute quantities. Inside the chocolate, the enzymes digest the starch and turn it into sweet, runny substances that are a delight to eat. Without the enzyme the paste would not taste as good.

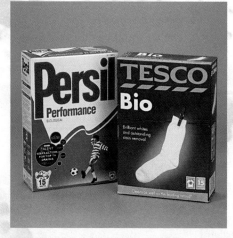

Figure 2 *Enzymes are used in soap powders.*

Questions

1 a) What is the most important factor that affects the food taken on space missions? *[Total 1]*

2 Where does the water come from on the space shuttle? *[Total 1]*

3 a) What professional person must agree the food of the astronauts? *[1]*
   b) What types of nutrients must be in the diet? *[5]*
   [Total 6]

4 Explain why enzymes are useful in industry. *[Total 3]*

5 What do you think is meant by 'an immobilised enzyme'? *[Total 2]*

6 Write out a flow chart of the processes for making lactose-free milk. *[Total 3]*

7 Describe how a runny centre can be made inside a solid chocolate. *[Total 2]*

Questions

1 Grass does not grow very well in the shade of large trees because it is in competition. Give three reasons why the grass only grows slowly. *[Total 3]*

2 The leaf is sometimes compared with a factory. Describe what you have to put into a leaf and what you get out. *[Total 5]*

3 Compare the different structures and functions of palisade cells and xylem vessels. *[Total 6]*

4 Describe two ways that small soluble substances can be absorbed into the blood. *[Total 4]*

5 Match the labels on Figure 1 with their name and function from the following list. Identify the part using the letter. *[Total 20]*

Name	Function
stomach	produces the enzyme amylase to start the digestion of starch
small intestine	produces bile to break down the fats in the diet
salivary gland	absorbs water from undigested remains of the food
gall bladder	crush the food into small manageable lumps
anus	produces acid to kill micro-organisms
liver	
pancreas	where faeces leaves the body
large intestine (colon)	temporary store of bile
teeth	has large surface area for absorption into the blood
rectum	produces enzymes to digest starch, protein and fat

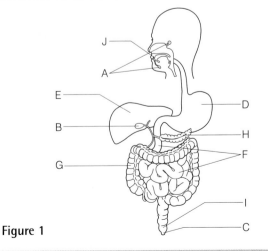

Figure 1

6 Frederick Gowland-Hopkins investigated the need for vitamins in the early twentieth century. He did the following experiment. Young rats were fed on a diet of pure milk protein, starch, sugar, lard and mineral salts for 18 days. A control group was fed on the same amount of each but each day 3 cm³ of milk was added. The mass of the rats was recorded. The two groups were then fed on the opposite diet for a further 30 days. The results are shown in Figure 2.

a) What was in the milk that helped the growth of the rats? *[1]*

b) Which of the group of substances in part a) is most likely to be responsible for the difference in growth? *[1]*

c) State a conclusion for the experiment. *[1]*

d) Suggest why the without milk treatment was swapped between groups after 18 days. *[2]*

e) Suggest other factors that Gowland-Hopkins would need to keep the same between the two groups of rats. *[3]*

[Total 8]

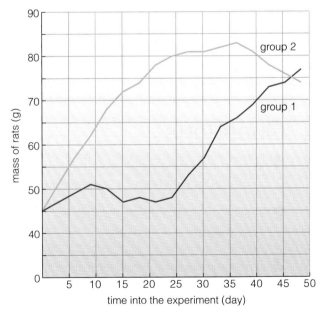

Figure 2

7 A trailing nasturtium plant was seen to be growing in bright sunshine but parts of the same stem was also entwined in a hedge. The light level was recorded for each of the leaves in the different positions. The leaves were taken and samples of each cut with a cork borer. 3 cm² was taken from each leaf and the amount of starch in each sample found. The leaf discs were crushed in a mortar and pestle, 5 cm³ of iodine solution added, the mixture filtered and the filtrate put into a colorimeter. The absorbance of the blue-black colour was measured. The results are shown in Table 1.

Light (lux)	3000	2500	2400	1500	900	850	750
Absorbance (%)	80	83	76	55	24	20	22

Table 1

a) Plot the data on graph paper using suitable axes. [8]
b) Explain why the leaf samples were ground in a mortar and pestle. [2]
c) Why was iodine solution used? [1]
d) What did the blue-black colour show? [1]
e) Make a conclusion from the data. [1]
f) Suggest how might this not be a fair test? [2]
[Total 15]

8 Describe why we have different shapes of teeth.
[Total 2]

9 What causes tooth decay? [Total 3]

10 Name two substances in saliva and what their functions are. [Total 4]

11 R Find out good sources of protein are available to:
a) a vegetarian
b) a vegan?

12 R Find out the nutrients in different foods to plan a menu for a day making sure there is the RDA for each nutrient.

13 R Try to find out where a plant stores the products of photosynthesis. What types of chemicals are produced.

14 R Find out the menus available for the International Space Station from the NASA web site.

15 P How would you investigate the prediction that more light produces more bubbles from a piece of pondweed?

16 P How could you investigate the prediction that 40 °C is the best temperature for the protease enzyme pepsin to digest egg white?

Releasing energy

3.1 Respiration

Oxygen and energy rich chemicals like glucose are taken into the body but how does the cell get the energy it needs to work?

Use of energy

One of the characteristics of living organisms is **respiration**, the release of chemical energy in cells. Cells use the energy for all their reactions and processes. These processes include:

- movement – muscle contraction.
- making new chemicals from small molecules, e.g. proteins from amino acids.
- growth and repair – putting together chemicals to make new cells or to replace old cells.
- active transport – moving substances through a cell membrane against a concentration gradient.
- nervous impulses – energy is needed for nerve cells to pass impulses along their length.
- heat – to keep mammals and birds at a constant body temperature.

Plants also need energy for all the processes listed above, except for movement and nervous impulses.

Respiration

All organisms must have a source of energy. Animals eat food containing energy rich chemicals like fat and starch. The chemicals are broken down by the digestive system into smaller molecules such as glucose. The digested molecules are absorbed into cells. Respiration takes place in the cytoplasm of cells. In the cytoplasm glucose is broken down to give carbon dioxide and water. This process also releases energy.

Plants get their energy from light and can use some of it straight away. Most of the light energy is transferred to the energy rich chemicals of glucose and starch. These substances are broken down and are used to release energy when the plant needs it. Plants need energy as much as animals do. Plants and animals need to release energy for cell reactions. The process of respiration occurs all the time in plants, just as it does in animals.

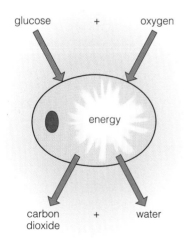

Figure 1.1

The reactions inside the cells need **enzymes** to carry them out. The enzymes help to control when the energy is released. If a cell does not need much energy, the enzymes are stopped from working.

Aerobic respiration

Aerobic respiration means the release of energy using oxygen. Oxygen is carried by the blood in animals and diffuses into cells. Glucose also travels to the cells in the blood. In plants the sugars are carried in phloem tissue. The phloem is found in the veins of the leaves and stem. Oxygen diffuses to all of the cells from the surface of the plant.

In the cytoplasm of cells there are specialised organelles called **mitochondria** which contain the enzymes needed for respiration. Oxygen diffuses into the mitochondria and is used to react with glucose to produce carbon dioxide and water. The chemical energy is transferred to a substance called ATP (adenosine triphosphate). For every one molecule of glucose broken down, 31 molecules of ATP are made. Each molecule of ATP has a small amount of energy. The ATP can move around the cell to take the small packets of energy to all the reactions that need it. The word equation for aerobic respiration is:

glucose + oxygen → carbon dioxide + water + (energy)

When the glucose molecules are broken down inside a cell, some of the chemical energy cannot be transferred into ATP. About 60% of the energy is given off as heat. This is why your muscles get warm when they are working hard. All organisms give off heat to the environment.

Anaerobic respiration

Anaerobic respiration is the release of energy *without* oxygen. If a person runs very quickly then breathing might not bring in enough oxygen. The person still needs to move so the muscle cells short cut the respiration process. The glucose is only partly broken down but this happens very quickly. Only a little of the energy can be transferred to the ATP. Most of the energy is left in the remaining substance which is called lactic acid.

The word equation for anaerobic respiration in a muscle is:

> ! You can test for carbon dioxide from respiration using limewater. If it becomes cloudy, then there was carbon dioxide in the air that was bubbled through it.

3.2 Breathing

You need to breathe to get oxygen. Oxygen is needed to release energy from food but how does breathing happen? Breathing can be divided into two parts. **Ventilation** is getting the air into and out of the lungs and **gas exchange** is getting the gases to move into or out of the blood. Gas exchange is a two-way process: waste gases are removed and oxygen is absorbed.

Ventilation in humans involves the movement of air through the nose or mouth, down the windpipe and into the lungs (inhaling). When you inhale the **diaphragm** contracts and flattens. The **rib muscles** move the ribs outwards and upwards. When the diaphragm and rib muscles contract, the volume in the chest increases so the air pressure in the lungs goes down. It goes below the atmospheric air pressure. Air rushes from the higher pressure outside the mouth into the area of lower pressure inside the lungs.

Figure 2.1 *Breathing system and lungs.*

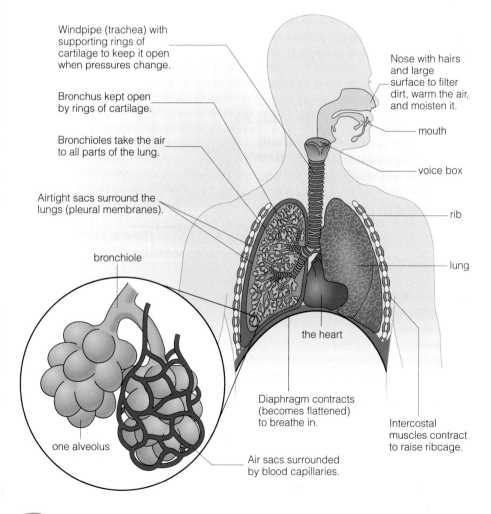

Windpipe (trachea) with supporting rings of cartilage to keep it open when pressures change.

Bronchus kept open by rings of cartilage.

Bronchioles take the air to all parts of the lung.

Airtight sacs surround the lungs (pleural membranes).

bronchiole

one alveolus

Air sacs surrounded by blood capillaries.

Nose with hairs and large surface to filter dirt, warm the air, and moisten it.

mouth

voice box

rib

lung

the heart

Diaphragm contracts (becomes flattened) to breathe in.

Intercostal muscles contract to raise ribcage.

To get the air out of the lungs again (exhaling), both the rib and diaphragm muscles relax. The ribs move down and in. The diaphragm returns to a dome shape making the volume of the chest smaller. This makes the air pressure in the lungs higher. The air is pushed out of the lungs.

The tissues of the lungs are elastic and recoil after being stretched like an elastic band. The elastic recoil helps the exhalation of the air. The lungs naturally return to the smaller, deflated, state.

In the lungs, gases can **diffuse** between the air and the blood. This gas exchange depends on the concentrations of each gas in the **alveoli** of the lungs and the concentration in the blood. The gases always move from where there is more of it (higher concentration) to where there is less (lower concentration). Table 2.1 shows typical concentrations of the gases. The difference in concentrations means that oxygen diffuses from the alveoli into the blood and carbon dioxide diffuses from the blood into the alveoli. This movement of the gases is called gas exchange. The changed air is then exhaled by the process of ventilation (breathing out).

Gas	Air entering lungs (%)	Blood entering lungs (% of saturation)
oxygen	20	10.6
carbon dioxide	0.03	58.0

Table 2.1 *Composition of gases in alveoli and blood.*

The diffusion depends on three factors.

⦾ Large surface area. The larger the surface area, the more gas can diffuse. Breathing in deeper lets the air get to more alveoli and therefore more oxygen can diffuse into the blood.
⦾ Short distance. The walls of the alveoli and capillaries (tiny blood vessels) must be very thin and close together so diffusion can happen as quickly as possible. The lining cells of the alveoli and capillaries are flattened like cheek cells but are even thinner (about 0.001 mm).
⦾ Diffusion gradient. Diffusion happens faster when there is a bigger difference in concentrations. Breathing replenishes the oxygen in the alveoli and the blood flow takes the oxygenated blood away. This maintains a large difference in concentration between the gases in the alveoli and in the blood.

The breathing system is designed to make sure the gases are exchanged at the rate they are needed. If more oxygen is needed by muscles because we are exercising, then the ventilation (breathing) rate goes up to increase the gas exchange. If the person rests then the breathing rate slows down.

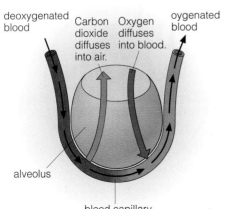

deoxygenated blood — Carbon dioxide diffuses into air. — Oxygen diffuses into blood. — oygenated blood

alveolus

blood capillary

Figure 2.2 *Alveolus and blood capillary showing diffusion of gases.*

> **!** Opera singers or anyone who trains their voice, can delicately control the flow of air to produce long notes from the voice box. The muscles between each rib and the stomach muscles give small contractions needed for the control.

> **!** The muscles controlling breathing are under automatic as well as conscious control. This means that you will always breathe even if you are asleep.

> **!** The surface area of the lungs is about 70 m², the size of a tennis court. This is made of 700 million alveoli and is between 30 and 40 times the area of the skin.

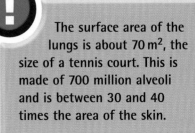

Smoking

Breathing in substances other than fresh air causes harm to the breathing system. Smoke from tobacco causes many problems.

The smoke contains particles that irritate the lungs as well as thousands of different chemicals. The medical effects of the smoke are shown in Figure 2.3. The nicotine in cigarettes is addictive. Smokers cannot get as much oxygen into the blood or remove as much carbon dioxide. They cannot be as active as if they could if they did not smoke.

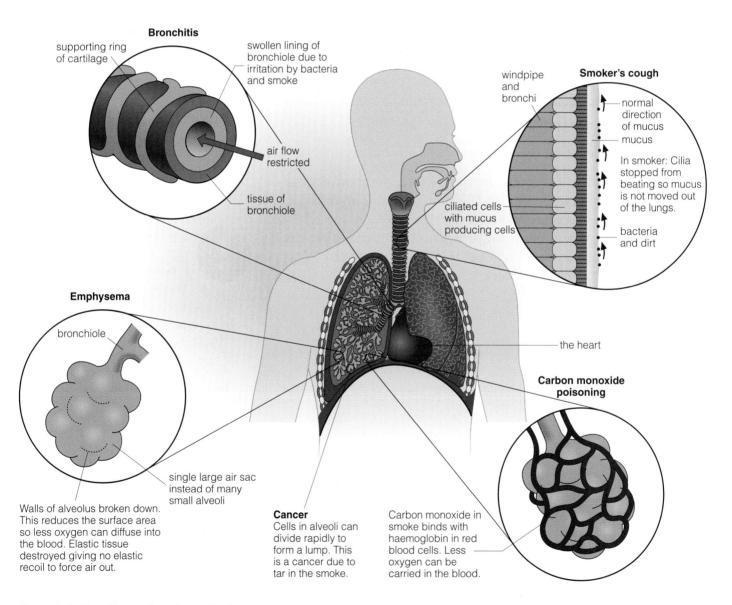

Bronchitis

supporting ring of cartilage

swollen lining of bronchiole due to irritation by bacteria and smoke

air flow restricted

tissue of bronchiole

windpipe and bronchi

Smoker's cough

normal direction of mucus

mucus

In smoker: Cilia stopped from beating so mucus is not moved out of the lungs.

bacteria and dirt

ciliated cells with mucus producing cells

Emphysema

bronchiole

the heart

single large air sac instead of many small alveoli

Walls of alveolus broken down. This reduces the surface area so less oxygen can diffuse into the blood. Elastic tissue destroyed giving no elastic recoil to force air out.

Cancer
Cells in alveoli can divide rapidly to form a lump. This is a cancer due to tar in the smoke.

Carbon monoxide poisoning

Carbon monoxide in smoke binds with haemoglobin in red blood cells. Less oxygen can be carried in the blood.

Figure 2.3 *The effects of smoke on the lungs.*

Asthma

Asthma develops when the bronchial tubes become swollen or inflamed. The muscles around the tubes contract to make the tubes narrow or the tubes are partly blocked by mucus. The narrowing of the tubes causes wheezy breathing.

The tubes usually narrow because of an allergy to house dust including house mite faeces. The faeces irritate the lining cells of the bronchi. The body reacts by getting a type of white blood cell to destroy the lining cells. The lining becomes swollen. Mucus, produced by the lining cells, becomes thicker and is not removed from the lungs. The mucus starts to block the airways.

The drugs in inhalers make the muscles around the bronchi relax so that the tubes open and it is easier to breathe. They do not cure the disease.

Gas exchange in plants

Plants also need to exchange gases. They need oxygen for respiration in the same way as animals but they also need carbon dioxide for photosynthesis.

Plants exchange the gases in their leaves. The air outside the leaf is free to move into the air spaces inside the leaf, through **stomata**. When the plant is photosynthesising, the carbon dioxide diffuses into the **mesophyll** leaf cells and oxygen diffuses out. In respiration the oxygen diffuses into the cells and carbon dioxide diffuses out. We notice this most when the plant is not photosynthesising i.e. when it is dark.

Figure 2.4 *The inhaler puts a very fine spray of a chemical around the air tubes inside the lungs, to make the muscles relax. This relieves the patient of the immediate problem and makes breathing easier.*

> **!** Asthma is not a recent disease. The word asthma comes from the Greek ($\alpha\sigma\theta\mu\alpha$) meaning 'short drawn breath'.

	Light (daytime)	Dark (night-time)
process	more photosynthesis than respiration	respiration only
oxygen	moves out of plant	moves into plant
carbon dioxide	moves into plant	moves out of plant

Table 2.2 *Gas exchange in plants.*

The leaf has a similar design to human lungs as there is a large surface area for diffusion inside the leaf and a short distance for the gases to move.

In a plant, the stem uses very little energy and so does not need much oxygen. The roots, buds and flowers have their own stomata to allow the gases to get to the cells. If the soil is full of water, all the air is pushed out. The roots of the plant cannot get oxygen for respiration. They cannot control the movement of the mineral salts into the plant and the plant may die.

Plants like the common rush *(Juncus squarrosus)* which live in boggy ground survive because they have special star shaped cells in the middle of the stem and root to keep the cells apart. This allows the air to move down to the roots from inside the plants. The oxygen is used by the root cells.

air space to take air into roots

Figure 2.5 *Common rush grows well in waterlogged ground.*

Summary

- Breathing is separated into ventilation and gas exchange.
- Air is moved into the lungs by contraction of diaphragm and rib muscles.
- Lung tissue is elastic to allow stretching and recoil for breathing out.
- Air moves through the nose or mouth, windpipe, bronchus, bronchiole, and into the alveoli.
- Diffusion of gases is made quicker by a large surface area, short distance and steeper diffusion gradient.
- Ciliated cells remove the mucus and trapped dirt or bacteria out of the bronchi and windpipe.
- Smoking causes heart disease, cancer, bronchitis and emphysema.
- Asthma is due to the narrowing of the air passages.
- Gases diffuse into and out of plant leaves through stomata.
- Carbon dioxide diffuses into the leaf in bright light and out of the leaf in darkness.

Questions

1 Copy and complete the following sentences.
The movement of air into and out of the lungs is called _____. The air movement is caused by pressure differences between the _____ in the lungs and the atmosphere. The _____ and rib muscles cause the ventilation. Oxygen diffuses into the blood and carbon dioxide _____ out. The alveoli in the lungs have very _____ walls to allow quick diffusion. The _____ carries the oxygen to all parts of the body. *[Total 3]*

2 Explain briefly why you need to breathe. *[Total 1]*

3 Briefly explain what is meant by:
a) ventilation *[1]*
b) gas exchange. *[1]*
[Total 2]

4 What is the difference between inhalation and exhalation? *[Total 2]*

5 Describe how the structure of the lungs makes gas exchange quick and efficient. *[Total 3]*

6 A smoker's cough is a deep clearing cough usually in the morning when the person first wakes up. It is caused because the cilia have worked and cleared some of the mucus with particles nearer to the throat. A cough clears some of the mucus. Use information about smoke to explain why the person stops coughing later in the day. *[Total 2]*

7 Explain why it is hard to breathe out during an asthma attack. *[Total 2]*

8 Match up the two halves of the sentence. Write out each full sentence. *[Total 4]*

Oxygen diffuses into the blood	in the blood.
Carbon dioxide is carried to the lungs	when there is a higher concentration in the lungs and a lower concentration in the blood.
In the dark, carbon dioxide	diffuses into a leaf.
When a plant photosynthesises the carbon dioxide	diffuses out of a leaf.

9 The gas contents of air and blood were measured to find out which gases were being used by the student. The results are shown in Table 2.3.
a) Which air sample contains the most oxygen? *[1]*
b) Which blood sample contains the most oxygen? *[1]*
c) Give a conclusion about the movement of oxygen. *[1]*
d) Which air sample contains the most carbon dioxide? *[1]*
e) Which blood sample contains the most carbon dioxide? *[1]*
f) Give a conclusion about the movement of carbon dioxide. *[1]*
g) Suggest why the nitrogen concentration remained the same for both the air and the blood. *[1]*
[Total 7]

Gas	Inhaled air (%)	Exhaled air (%)	Blood entering lungs (cm^3 per 100 cm^3)	Blood leaving lungs (cm^3 per 100 cm^3)
oxygen	21	16	10	19
carbon dioxide	0.03	4	58	50
nitrogen	79	79	0.9	0.9

Table 2.3

Arteries	Capillaries	Veins
carry blood away from heart	carry blood through organs and tissues	carry blood towards heart
blood at high pressure	blood at low pressure	blood at lowest pressure
no valves	no valves	valves to stop blood flowing back
thick muscular walls	very thin walls for escape of fluids	thinner walls with less muscle
no substances leave or enter vessel	exchange of substances with tissues	no substances leave or enter vessel
pulse created by heart pumping and contraction of wall muscle	no pulse	no pulse
strong walls	delicate and easily broken	flexible and squashed easily so blood pushed further along vessel

Table 3.1 *Differences between types of blood vessel.*

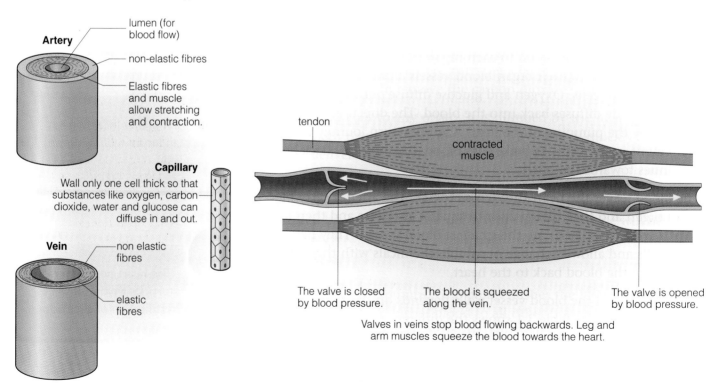

Artery
lumen (for blood flow)
non-elastic fibres
Elastic fibres and muscle allow stretching and contraction.

Capillary
Wall only one cell thick so that substances like oxygen, carbon dioxide, water and glucose can diffuse in and out.

Vein
non elastic fibres
elastic fibres

tendon
contracted muscle

The valve is closed by blood pressure.
The blood is squeezed along the vein.
The valve is opened by blood pressure.

Valves in veins stop blood flowing backwards. Leg and arm muscles squeeze the blood towards the heart.

Figure 3.3 *Blood vessels.*

Figure 3.4 *Longitudinal section of vein.*

Blood

There are about 5 litres of blood in an average adult person and it makes one complete circuit of the body about once a minute, i.e. two passes through the heart, one through the lungs and once to one of the organs.

Blood is about 50% water and 50% cells by volume. Most of the cells are red because they contain the substance **haemoglobin**. These **red blood cells** are specialised: their function is to carry oxygen from the lungs to the tissues. They do not have a nucleus so the cell can contain more haemoglobin. Each blood cell is made in the bone marrow and only lasts for about four months as it travels round the body. Worn out or damaged red cells are destroyed by the liver. If the haemoglobin has been poisoned by carbon monoxide the whole red blood cell is destroyed. People who smoke have fewer working red blood cells to carry the oxygen because of the carbon monoxide they inhale.

White blood cells have the task of fighting disease. There are about 500 times fewer white blood cells than red blood cells. White blood cells are divided into different types, each with a special function. For example, the **phagocytes** can engulf a bacterium by moving around it and enclosing it. The phagocyte then digests the bacterium inside the cell. If many phagocytes have gone to one point in the skin to get rid of invading bacteria they form the white pus that you see in spots.

Other white blood cells called lymphocytes produce antibodies which are released into the blood plasma. Antibodies are chemicals which are specially produced to destroy just one type of invader. They help the body to kill a bacterium or a virus. If that type of bacterium invades the body again the same antibody can be produced more rapidly than before. The person is then immune to the bacterium.

A very small type of cell without a nucleus, (called a blood **platelet**) helps the blood to clot. Clotting is very important to stop bleeding and prevent micro-organisms entering the body.

The liquid part of the blood is called **plasma**. It is water with many substances dissolved in it making it a pale yellow colour. Plasma carries small molecules such as glucose, amino acids and vitamins from the diet as well as hormones and heat. It is very important for the muscles and nerve cells to be given glucose as well as oxygen, so that they have a steady supply of energy. The waste products carbon dioxide and urea (from waste protein) are also carried in the plasma.

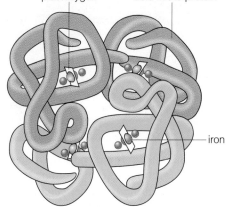

haem group plus oxygen | chains of amino acid in the protein

iron

Figure 3.5 *Haemoglobin molecule showing the need for iron and the carriage of oxygen. Haemoglobin is a type of protein.*

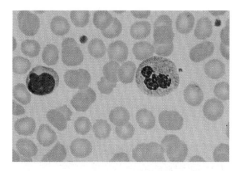

Figure 3.6 *Red and white blood cells. The red cells are thinner in the centre so have a lighter colour there. They do not have a nucleus. The white cells have a nucleus which has been stained to show up in the photograph.*

Figure 3.7 *The heart during an operation. The blood vessels feeding the heart muscle itself can be seen. These are the ones that can be blocked in a heart attack.*

Health problems of the heart and blood vessels

Heart attacks are caused by a blockage in a coronary artery (the blood vessels going to the muscular wall of the heart). The heart muscle does not get enough oxygen or glucose. That part of the heart muscle stops working so the whole heart cannot beat properly. The blockage can be caused by a blood clot getting stuck in a narrowed artery.

Nicotine from cigarette smoke makes the blood more likely to form clots. Too much fat in the diet causes a type of fat called cholesterol to be left on the inside of the arteries (atheroma). This makes them narrower and so a blood clot is more likely to get trapped.

A first aider will give cardiac compressions to the chest to squash the heart and so make the blood move around the body.

High salt in the diet causes the heart to beat faster the blood pressure increases and the blood vessels become less flexible. The higher blood pressure causes more fluid to be pushed out of the capillaries. The person is often heavier than necessary due to the extra fluid carried.

Angina is the first sign of heart disease with several of the arteries becoming narrower. A sharp pain develops in the left arm and the person gets tired much more quickly than they should.

A **stroke** happens when there is a blood clot in the blood vessels of the brain. The person becomes confused and usually becomes unconscious. Permanent damage to the brain can occur but a person can completely recover from the first stroke.

Summary

- A circulation system carries substances around the body and helps to fight against disease.
- Humans have a double circulation system, one to the lungs and one to the body.
- The heart acts as a pump for the blood to carry oxygen, nutrients, waste substances and hormones.
- Arteries carry blood away from the heart and veins carry blood towards the heart.
- Capillaries are found in the tissues, are very narrow and allow exchange of substances.
- Haemoglobin in red blood cells carries the oxygen.
- Blood platelets help clot the blood.
- White blood cells fight disease.
- Heart attacks occur when the heart stops pumping.
- Strokes occur due to a blood clot in the brain.

Questions

1 Copy and complete the following sentences. Blood is pumped by the _____ The blood leaves the heart through _____. It goes to the _____ of the body where exchange of substances can occur. The _____ blood vessels are called capillaries. They have very thin walls to let the substances _____ in or out. The blood returns to the _____ in veins. Oxygen is carried in _____ blood cells by haemoglobin. A person with a high fat diet is likely to have _____ arteries. A blood _____ is more likely to form and get stuck at the narrowed point. If it happens in the _____ muscle the person may have a heart attack. *[Total 5]*

2 How many chambers does the human heart have? *[Total 1]*

3 a) What makes the valves in the heart shut? *[1]*
b) Why do they need to do this? *[1]*
[Total 2]

4 Explain why the left side of the heart has thicker muscle than the right side. *[Total 1]*

5 Explain what is meant by 'double circulation'. *[Total 2]*

6 Where are red blood cells made? *[Total 1]*

7 What substance can poison red blood cells? *[Total 1]*

8 Copy and complete Table 3.2. *[Total 5]*

Artery	Capillary	Vein
carries blood from the heart	blood flows from arteries to veins	
very thick wall consisting of muscle		thinner wall with no muscle
	blood flows slowly	blood flows slowly
can feel pulse	no pulse	
no valves		valves to stop blood flowing back

Table 3.2

9 Describe the flow of blood from a leg muscle to the heart and lungs and back to the muscle listing each organ the blood travels through and what happens at each place. *[Total 8]*

10 What type of cell helps to form blood clots? *[Total 1]*

11 Explain the following conditions:
a) a heart attack *[3]*
b) a stroke *[2]*
c) atheroma. *[2]*
[Total 7]

12 What makes the human circulation system so efficient at carrying oxygen to the tissues? *[Total 3]*

History

Round in circles – the development of ideas for blood circulation

Ideas in science develop over a long period of time. Careful observation and investigations are needed. Many scientists are often involved but it is William Harvey who is always associated with the 'discovery' of circulation of the blood.

During the Roman Empire the philosopher Galen (born about AD 130) was the first to describe the organs of the body. He thought that the liver was the centre of the circulation system and that the heart regulated the flow and cooled the blood by the chest movements. He wrote, 'Smoky vapours from the heart were given out'. Galen believed that blood passed from the right side to the left side of the heart through invisible pores in the dividing wall. Religious beliefs stopped further observations until the Renaissance period when a Belgian scientist called Andreas Vesalius (1514–1563) made careful observations.

Vesalius said that the blood could not pass from the right to the left side of the heart but he did not provide another idea. He still thought that Galen's idea about the importance of the liver in the flow of blood was correct. Vesalius lost his job at the University of Padua (Italy) because of his ideas.

In 1553, a Spanish theologian and physician called Servetus wrote a book that included the idea that the blood must go through the lungs to get from the right to the left side of the heart. He died at the stake because he preached ideas which did not agree with the teachings of the Catholic Church.

Gerolamo Fabrizio d'Aquapendente (called Fabricius) (1533–1619) also worked at Padua and described the operation of valves in veins to show one-way flow. However, he got the direction wrong believing the blood flowed away from the heart in the veins. Fabricius was one of the tutors for the Englishman William Harvey (1578–1657) who is credited with the discovery of the circulation system.

Harvey was the first to collect all the observations together and add his own evidence. His work *Exercitatio anatomica de motu cordis et sanguinus in animalibus* (anatomical study concerning the heart and blood in animals) was published in 1628. He described the heart as a pump. The chambers were filled during the resting phase and then the muscles contracted to force the blood out. The blood flowed from the left

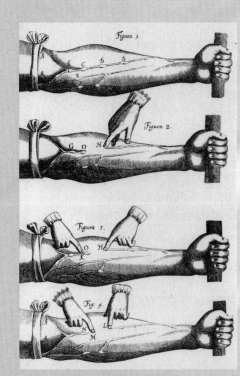

Figure 1 *Diagram from Harvey's book. It shows valves in the veins only allowing blood to flow back up the arm.*

ventricle, through the aorta to the different organs of the body. Somehow it then got to the veins where it returned to the heart. The valves and direction of flow were correctly observed and the evidence of swelling of the veins by the valves was described (Figure 1).

Harvey described the return of the blood to the right side of the heart followed by movement to the lungs where it was turned into arterial blood. By this he meant oxygenated. It was not until later that John Mayow (1643–1679), who was born in Cornwall, carried out a simple experiment to show the oxygenation of blood. He passed air through venous blood. It became bright red like arterial blood. This confirmed Harvey's idea of the connections in the lungs. The idea that oxygen was needed by the body and carried in the blood was not realised until a century later, after the work of Priestley and Lavoisier, who discovered the element.

Figure 2 *Teaching anatomy.*

In 1660, Marcello Malphighi managed to see minute vessels with blood flowing through them (capillaries). He used a simple microscope and the wing of a bat to see the tiny vessels in the thin membrane of the wing. This completed the evidence needed for Harvey's ideas about the circulation of blood.

Questions

1 a) What did Galen think was the centre of the circulation system? [1]
   b) What role did Galen find for the heart? [1]
   c) How did Galen think the blood got from the right side of the heart to the left? [1]
   [Total 3]

2 Name the scientist who first thought that the blood could not pass from the right to the left side of the heart. [Total 1]

3 How did Servetus suggest that the blood could get from the right to the left side of the heart? [Total 1]

4 a) How did Harvey describe the heart? [1]
   b) What did Harvey consider to be the role of:
   i) the arteries
   ii) the veins? [2]
   c) What did Harvey think was the function of the valves in the veins? [1]
   [Total 4]

5 a) Which type of blood vessel was the last to be discovered? [1]
   b) What needed to be invented before the smallest type of blood vessel was discovered? [1]
   [Total 2]

6 Suggest a reason why some scientists do not want to publish their results. [Total 1]

Figure 1

Applications

Athletics and training

When an athlete runs, the small store of ATP in their muscles is used up quickly. More energy must be released by respiration. The available stores of oxygen and energy rich compounds in the muscles start to be used up. New supplies must be taken to the muscles by the blood system. If the muscles need more energy than can be released with the supply of oxygen, then anaerobic respiration occurs.

The amount of carbohydrate (energy supply) stored in the muscles can be increased if the athlete trains until exhausted and then eats a high carbohydrate diet. The muscle gets better at absorbing glucose and converting it into the storage carbohydrate, glycogen. The glycogen can be used to supply energy because it is broken down into glucose and used in respiration. The person does not get as tired as quickly and carries on at higher speeds for longer. Taking sports drinks with glucose in them can help to increase performance. The water in the drink stops athletes getting dehydrated and they can keep on cooling the body by sweating.

Too much fat in the diet stops the muscle cells taking up glucose from the blood and makes the cells slower to release energy needed. Exercising muscles helps them to grow. The recommended normal amount of protein in the diet is enough for the muscles to grow and be stronger.

If not enough oxygen is provided during exercise, anaerobic respiration occurs until the muscles poison themselves with lactic acid. Short duration, 'explosive' events can allow anaerobic respiration to be the main source of energy. A top class sprinter running a 100 m race may not breathe at all during the race (Table 1).

Table 1 *Summary of approximate oxygen needs of winning athletes in different kinds of events.*

Event	Total energy expended (kJ)	Oxygen needed (dm^3)	Oxygen breathed in (dm^3)	Oxygen debt (dm^3)	% of energy from aerobic respiration	% of energy from anaerobic respiration
100 m	200	10	0–0.5	9.5–10	0–5	95–100
1500 m	720	36	19	17	55	45
42 186 m (marathon)	14 000	700	685	15	98	2

A person running a marathon trains so they do not build up any lactic acid until the last moments of the race. Their speed is limited by the ability of the circulation system to get oxygen to the muscles and release energy (see Table 1). The last lap of a race or last few minutes is when the marathon runner can run faster.

Training for athletics can help the body do the following:

- increase glucose uptake into muscle cells from the blood
- increase the storage of glycogen (carbohydrate energy) in the muscle cells
- increase tolerance of the muscles to lactic acid – they can carry on working with more lactic acid in them
- increase the strength of the heart muscle and skeletal muscles
- increase the volume of blood that can be pumped out of the heart at one beat (stroke volume)
- increase the number of red blood cells in the blood
- increase the depth and rate of breathing for more gas exchange.

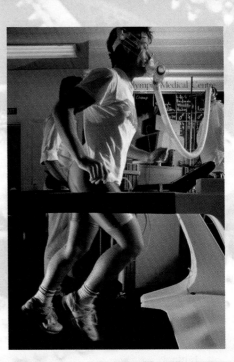

Figure 2

Questions

1 Suggest why a high protein diet does not improve performance for marathon runners. *[Total 2]*

2 Explain how the following allow a better performance by athletes:
a) greater number of red blood cells *[2]*
b) greater store of glycogen in the muscles *[1]*
c) increased tolerance of muscles to lactic acid *[1]*
d) taking in liquids during a marathon race. *[1]*
[Total 5]

3 Which type of athletic race receives the greatest proportion of energy from:
a) anaerobic respiration *[1]*
b) aerobic respiration? *[1]*
[Total 2]

4 According to Table 1, 1500 m runners show the highest oxygen debt.
a) How does an oxygen debt form? *[1]*
b) Suggest why 1500 m runners develop a greater oxygen debt than marathon runners. *[2]*
[Total 3]

5 What is meant by the term 'stroke volume'? *[Total 1]*

6 Suggest a training regime for you to become a better long distance runner. *[Total 4]*

Questions

1 Which of the following cell types would have more mitochondria. State your reason for the answer.

Human cheek cell   Muscle cell

Ciliated cell   Fat storage cell   *[Total 2 marks]*

2 Copy and complete the table to explain the differences between aerobic and anaerobic respiration in animals.

Feature	Aerobic respiration	Anaerobic respiration
gases used		
substances used		
gases produced		
other substances produced		
amount of energy released		

Table 1   *[Total 10 marks]*

3 Make a table to compare features of lungs and leaves for gas exchange.   *[Total 8 marks]*

4 Explain how emphysema makes it more difficult to breathe.   *[Total 2 marks]*

5 a) What is the commonest cause of asthma?   *[1]*

b) Treatment using the muscle relaxant in blue inhalers does not cure asthma. Explain the difference between stopping the signs of the asthma attack and curing the disease.   *[2]*

[Total 3 marks]

6 a) What is diffusion?   *[1]*

b) Describe how the diffusion gradient for oxygen from the alveolus to the blood is maintained.   *[2]*

[Total 3 marks]

7 Ben investigated his breathing rate during exercise. He used an exercise machine for 5 minutes and breath sensors. The results are recorded below.

Exercise rate	Volume of air per breath (cm^3)	Breaths per minute
at rest	400	20
during running	800	45
after running for 5 min	1000	32

Table 2

a) What is the total volume of air breathed in per minute :
 i) at rest
 ii) during running
 ii) after running for 5 min?   *[3]*

b) The difference in amount of oxygen between the air breathed in and out is 4%. Calculate how much oxygen is diffused into the blood per minute :-
 i) at rest
 ii) during running
 iii) after running   *[3]*

c) Ben felt tired after running. What type of respiration was occurring in their muscles towards the end of running?   *[1]*

d) Why is the amount of oxygen diffusing into the blood greater after running than at rest?   *[2]*

e) List 5 different uses of the energy released when Ben was at rest. For each one suggest how it allows the person to survive.   *[10]*

[Total 19 marks]

8 Draw a sketch diagram of the double circulation system of humans labelling the 'body', heart and lungs. On it colour the oxygenated blood bright red and the deoxygenated blood dark red. Label the arteries and veins.   *[Total 10 marks]*

9 Make a table of the different parts of the blood, a special feature of each part and the function that part does.   *[Total 12 marks]*

10 Copy and complete the table

Substance carried in plasma	Organ or tissue where substance enters the blood plasma	Organ or tissue where substance leaves the blood plasma
oxygen		all tissues
	all tissues	lungs
glucose		all tissues
	lymphocytes	all tissues

Table 3   *[Total 4 marks]*

11 State 2 foods produced using anaerobic respiration.   *[Total 2 marks]*

12 Explain why the following features are needed for efficient gas exchange:
  a) Rings of cartilage surround the windpipe and bronchi
  b) The lining cells of the alveolus are very thin
  c) The chest cavity is made air-tight by a pair of pleural membranes
  d) Air moves into the lungs when the space in the chest gets bigger
  e) The air sacs are elastic
  f) It is more difficult to breathe (ventilate the lungs) at high altitude (e.g. walking in the Himalayas) than at sea level.   *[Total 6 marks]*

13 R Find out how the oxygen is carried to the cells in insects and simple animals like sea anemones.

14 R Find out how whales are able to hold their breath for up to 112 minutes during a single dive.

15 R Find out how many people in the U.K. die each year from smoking related illness. What is the estimate of the cost of treating smoking diseases?

16 R A man has a heart attack. A first-aider gives 'cardiac pulmonary resuscitation'. How does the first-aider do the CPR and how will it save the man's life?

17 P Bread rises because of the respiration of yeast. What factors would affect the amount that bread might rise?

18 P How would you investigate the effect of increasing sugar concentration on the speed of respiration of a suspension of yeast?

19 P How would you investigate the effect of increasing rate of exercise on the breathing rate? [Write your answer as a series of bullet point statements. Include the terms input and outcome variables.]

Controlling life

4.1 Skeletons and movement

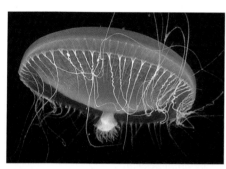

Why do you have a skeleton? Animals have a skeleton to support their bodies, and muscles that help them to move. Movement requires energy. Muscles use energy in the body to produce movement.

Skeleton

A skeleton provides support and protection. Animals like jellyfish and earthworms do not have a bony skeleton. However, jellyfish are supported by water around them. Earthworms are supported by water inside their bodies: this is called a hydrostatic skeleton. Animals with backbones are called **vertebrates** and have internal skeletons called **endoskeletons**. Animals like lobsters and insects, which are **invertebrates**, do not have a backbone. However, they have a tough outside or external skeleton, which is called an **exoskeleton**.

Exoskeletons provide good overall protection. The skeleton is like an armoured overcoat but as the animal grows, it needs to replace its exoskeleton. It sheds its tough protective outer skeleton, and a new larger skeleton takes its place. However, the new skeleton is soft to start with. During the shedding of the old skeleton and the hardening of the new one, the animal is extremely vulnerable to predators, because it has no protection.

The human **skeleton** is sometimes referred to as a framework. Without a skeleton we would be shapeless blobs. A skeleton has many similarities to the frame of a bicycle:

- both must be strong and light for easy movement.
- they are both structures made up of many parts.
- bones and bicycle frames tend to be tubes, which carry loads and transfer forces efficiently.

Figure 1.1 *Jellyfish have no skeleton. Locusts have an exoskeleton that they must shed as they grow.*

> **!** The backbone (vertebral column) is not the longest bone in the body. The backbone is actually 33 small bones joined. They protect the spinal cord. The longest bone in the skeleton is found in the thigh and the smallest is found in the ear.

Bones

There are 206 bones in the human skeleton. Some of the bones are hollow in the middle and contain a substance called **marrow**. This makes them extremely light and strong. The total weight of an adult skeleton is approximately 9 kg. Bone is a mixture of living tissue and non-living material. The living tissues contain cells and collagen fibres. The collagen allows the bones to be flexible. The non-living part of bone is made up of minerals and salts such as calcium phosphate. The calcium phosphate makes the bone hard. Without it the bone would be flexible like the cartilage found in the ear or in the end of the nose.

Bone growth occurs in children and adolescents. Growth takes place at the ends of the bones. If there is a shortage of calcium during a child's life then the bones remain soft and can become deformed. This is called **rickets**. In later life, adults whose bones lack calcium can develop brittle bones which break easily.

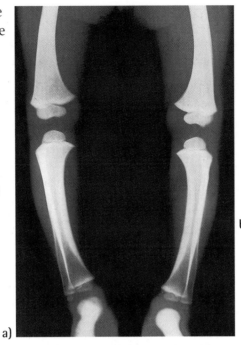
a)

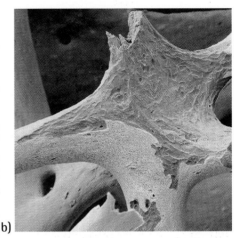
b)

Figure 1.2 **a)** *X-rays of bones of a child with rickets* **b)** *Brittle bones in an adult.*

Although bone is a strong material it can be broken. Breaks are repaired by the bone cells producing more collagen fibres and releasing more calcium phosphate. However, bone can also be strengthened during exercise. This is because extra fibres and calcium salts are added to the parts of the bone where most stress takes place.

The bones of the skeleton have four main functions:

◉ They provide *support*, which allows the body to stand upright.
◉ They give *protection* to many organs. For example the bones of the skull are joined together to make a strong box to protect the brain, and the ribs form a cage that protects the lungs and heart.
◉ Together with muscle they can produce *movement*.
◉ *Blood cells* are made in the bone marrow.

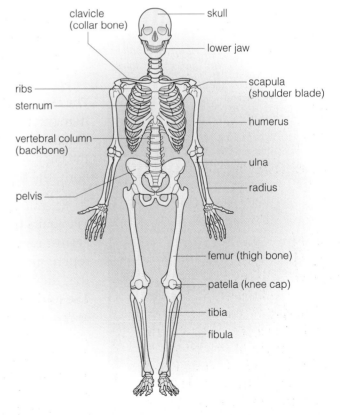

Figure 1.3

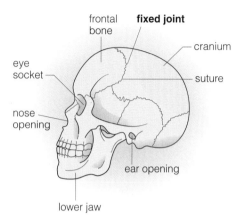

Figure 1.4 *Fixed joints in the skull.*

Joints

Different parts of the body need to move in different ways. A **joint** is a place where two bones meet. There are three types of joint:

- **Fixed joint**: bones meet but there is no movement. The bones of the skull demonstrate this.
- **Hinge joint**: the bones here move in only one direction, a good example is the knee joint.
- **Ball and socket joint**: the bones can swivel and move in any direction. One bone of the joint has a round end that fits into a round hole in the other bone, as in our shoulders and hips.

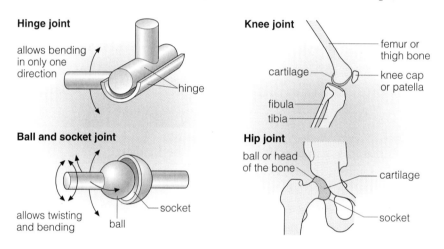

Figure 1.5 *Hinge and ball and socket joints.*

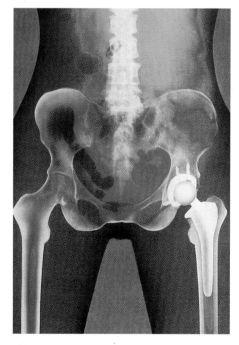

Figure 1.6 *X-ray of a hip joint replacement.*

The skull protects the brain and has joints. The bones grow joints where they meet. In a fetus the skull bones are not joined (fused). This is because during birth the bones of the skull move so that the head of the baby can be squashed and pass through the mother's pelvis. Once born, the baby has a hole in its skull called the **fontanelle**, or soft spot. The joints of the skull close up slowly to allow brain growth.

The joints that allow movement do so because the bones can slide against each other. The surface of the bones at the joints is covered in a tough, smooth substance called **cartilage**. This protects the bones so that they do not wear away. The cartilage also acts like a shock absorber. The joints are lubricated with a liquid called **synovial fluid**. The whole joint is wrapped by a **ligament** which is a flexible, elastic material.

Exercising regularly helps to keep joints working smoothly. As people get older the lubricating fluid in the joints may dry up. This may result in them suffering with diseases such as arthritis or rheumatism. The cartilage gets so worn down that the end of the bone cannot move freely and rubs together. The diseased joints become swollen and painful. Doctors are able to replace some diseased joints.

Movement

The bones of a skeleton cannot move on their own. The movement of joints is controlled by **muscles**. These are attached to the bones and can pull the bones into different positions.

Muscle is tissue that can contract and makes up part of the body. It is attached to bones by cords called **tendons**, which do not stretch. A muscle works by shortening and pulling. When this happens a muscle gets shorter. We can actually see our muscles working. As a muscle works it gets shorter or **contracts**. It becomes hard, looks fatter and bulges out more. A muscle can **relax** and stop pulling, but it cannot stretch and push on the bones to get the joint back to its original position. The bone must be pulled by another muscle. Muscles always work in pairs. Wherever there is one muscle there is another to work against it. This arrangement is known as an **antagonistic pair**.

The arrangement of the bones in a bird's wing is similar to the bones of a human arm. The bird's wing is moved by muscles. The flight muscles are large and powerful and are attached to the breast bone. There are two flight muscles. One pulls the wing up and the other pulls it down. The most powerful muscles are the ones that pull the wings down. Bird bones are extremely light.

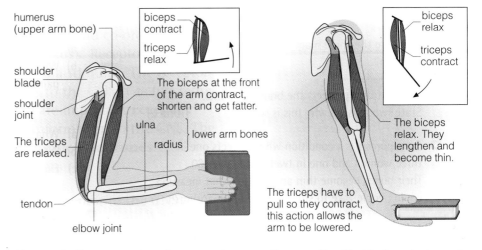

Figure 1.7 *The contraction of one muscle causes the opposite effect in its paired muscle.*

Summary

- An external skeleton provides protection and support, but it must be shed so that growth can occur.
- The major functions of the internal skeleton are to support and protect vital organs and aid movement.
- All moveable joints of the body have cartilage to protect the bones and synovial fluid to lubricate them.
- The bones of a joint are held together by ligaments.
- Muscles are attached to bones by tendons.
- Bones move because muscles contract and pull on the tendons.
- Muscles always work in pairs.

4.3 Hormones

Hormones are blamed for making teenagers moody! What are hormones? **Hormones** are chemicals that help us control our bodies. We have two control systems, the nervous system and hormonal system. Responses controlled by the nervous system are fast and are over quickly, e.g. muscle contraction. The responses that are controlled by hormones are slow but may last for a longer time. Plants also have a hormonal system, and plant growth is controlled by plant growth substances.

Hormones in animals

Hormones are soluble chemicals made by a number of glands that make up the **endocrine** system. An endocrine gland makes hormones and releases (or secretes) them directly into the bloodstream. Endocrine glands have a good blood capillary network inside. Hormones help us control organs inside our bodies and carry messages throughout the body. Not all organs in the body will respond to a hormone. Hormones affect specific organs called target organs. Most endocrine glands are controlled by the **pituitary** gland, which is at the base of the brain.

For the body to work properly, it needs to have the correct amount of each hormone. The pituitary gland is known as the master gland because it produces many hormones, which control and co-ordinate other hormones.

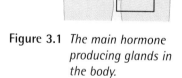

pituitary gland

thyroid gland

pancreas

adrenal gland

ovary (female)

testis (male)

Figure 3.1 *The main hormone producing glands in the body.*

The tallest person is caused by too much growth hormone, and some people of restricted growth have too little!

Figure 3.2

Specific examples of hormones

The **thyroid** gland is found in the neck, and secretes the hormone **thyroxin**. Thyroxin controls the body's **metabolism** and growth. Metabolism is the production of energy carried out inside cells. A person who secretes a lot of thyroxin becomes thin, excitable and over-active. A person with low levels of thyroxin secretion puts on weight as the metabolic rate slows down, and he or she becomes sluggish.

The **pancreas** secretes the hormone **insulin**, which controls the body's blood sugar levels. Insulin production is increased if there is too much sugar (glucose) in the blood. The insulin makes the liver take in the glucose and store it. (It is stored in the form of glycogen, which is a large molecule made of lots of small glucose molecules joined together.) This makes glucose levels fall back to normal. Most people have the correct blood sugar levels. People who suffer from the disease **diabetes** have too much sugar in their blood. They do not make enough insulin. Symptoms of diabetes include being very thirsty and not having very much energy. Diabetics can control their condition with regular injections of insulin and careful eating.

Preparing for action

The adrenal glands secrete the hormone **adrenaline**. Adrenaline prepares the body for action. Adrenaline causes an immediate response in the body. The adrenal glands only make a very small amount of adrenaline, but it has an instant and dramatic affect on the body. The rate and force of the heart beat increase, breathing rate increases and blood is directed away from the stomach towards the muscles. The effect is a rush of extra energy that helps to *fight* the stressful situation or *flee* and run away from it. Adrenaline is an unusual hormone because it acts very quickly but its effects do not last.

Hormones and the control of sexual development

The **testes** secrete the male sex hormone **testosterone**. Testosterone causes sexual development in males, e.g. production of sperm and the deepening of the voice. **Oestrogen** is the hormone that causes sexual development in females, e.g. the development of breasts and the widening of hips. The female sex hormones are secreted from the **ovaries**. The female sex hormones are also responsible for controlling the menstrual cycle.

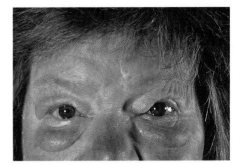

Figure 3.3 *Low levels of thyroxine secretion causes a low metabolic rate resulting in puffiness around the eyes.*

Figure 3.4 *Adrenaline in action.*

> **!** Hormones can be used in the treatment of diseases. Corticosteroids, which are made from cortisone (a hormone), are used to treat rheumatoid arthritis. The chemicals are made into a cream that can be rubbed on painful joints to reduce swelling.

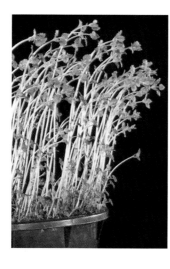

Hormones in plants

Plants are sensitive to different stimuli: light, moisture, gravity and touch. They do not respond to the stimuli by moving muscles, but by growing in a certain direction. The growing responses are called **tropisms**. Tropisms are controlled by plant growth substances. The main substances that control growth in plants are called **auxins**. Plant hormones are also known as plant growth substances.

Figure 3.5 *Plants grow towards the light.*

Tropisms

There are two main growth responses in plants. The response to light is called **phototropism**, and the response to gravity is called **geotropism**. Hormones are not spread evenly in the plant. Hormones are produced in the growing tips of shoots and transported in the phloem.

Auxin in shoots causes the cells to lengthen and grow. Auxin collects on the shaded side of the shoot. The cells therefore elongate. Light from one direction makes the shoot curve and grow towards the light. This is called **positive phototropism**. Roots grow in the direction of gravity (this is called positive geotropism), and are attracted to water in the soil.

> **!** Seedless grapes are produced with the help of hormones. The hormones allow the fruit to grow without fertilisation so there are no pips.

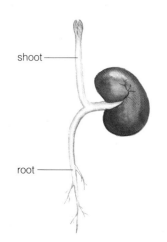

shoot

root

Figure 3.6 *A germinating seedling.*

> **!** Gardeners use hormone-rooting powder to encourage the growth of roots in stem cuttings.

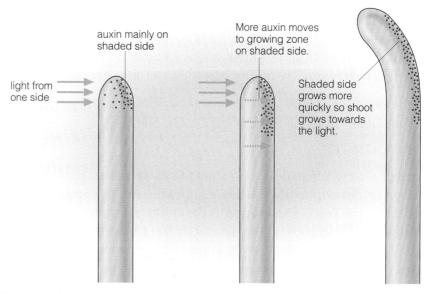

auxin mainly on shaded side

More auxin moves to growing zone on shaded side.

light from one side

Shaded side grows more quickly so shoot grows towards the light.

Figure 3.7 *Response of shoots to light.*

Summary

- Hormones are chemicals that control changes in the body.
- Hormones are transported in animals as a solution in the blood plasma.
- Examples of hormones in animals include insulin, adrenaline, testosterone, progesterone and oestrogen.
- Auxins are a group of plant hormones.
- The movement of shoots in the response to light is called phototropism.
- The movement of roots in the response to gravity is called geotropism.

Questions

1 Copy and complete the following sentences.
Hormones are _____, which are released by different glands. The glands make up the _____ system. Hormones act more slowly than the _____ system. _____ control responses in plants. Plant shoots grow towards _____ and the roots grow towards moisture and in the direction of _____. *[Total 3]*

2 a) What are hormones? *[2]*
b) Explain how hormones enter the blood. *[2]*
[Total 4]

3 The nervous system and the hormonal system control the sending of messages in the body differently. Describe two of these differences. *[Total 4]*

4 Harry and Stephen have just finished running, and both have a high sugar sports drink. Table 3.1 shows their blood glucose levels.
a) Plot a graph to show the changes for the two boys. *[5]*
b) Which boy has diabetes? *[1]*
c) Explain your answer *[1]*
[Total 7]

Time after drinking sports drink (min)	Blood glucose level (mg per 100 cm^3 blood)	
	Harry	**Stephen**
0	74	80
15	85	90
30	110	125
45	140	170
60	115	190
75	90	210
90	80	210
105	84	200
120	85	180
135	74	145

Table 3.1

5 Explain the role of auxin in plant growth. *[Total 1]*

6 Show with the use of diagrams the effect that gravity and light have on plants. *[Total 2]*

History

Anatomy and dissection

The fifteenth century artist Leonardo da Vinci (1452–1519) was fascinated with the natural world and the human body. He filled many notebooks with sketches, including drawings made by observing the human body. Da Vinci's famous anatomy drawings include a very detailed picture of the hand and another of the body called Vetruvian man. Vetruvian man was drawn in 1490. It shows exact anatomical proportions of a man.

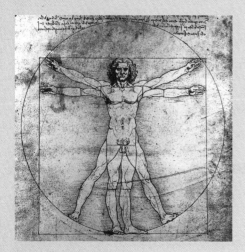

Figure 1 *Vetruvian man.*

Da Vinci could only study anatomy by dissecting bodies. Dissection means cutting bodies apart to study how they are organised. Dissection can also be carried out in surgery. However, in Europe in the Middle Ages, dissection was considered a sin.

In Britain at the end of the eighteenth century there was a great deal of scientific interest in anatomy. However, it was only legal to use the bodies of murderers who had been hanged for their crimes. This did not provide enough bodies for anatomists to work on. A trade started in dead bodies which had been removed from graves. William Burke and William Hare were notorious grave robbers. They worked in Edinburgh at the beginning of the nineteenth century. Burke and Hare first sold the body of an old man who had died from natural causes in their lodgings. They sold him to an anatomist to use for dissection. After that they began robbing graves for bodies. Eventually they started to murder people to increase the supply of bodies. They would lure victims to their lodgings, get them drunk and then smother (suffocate) them. They suffocated their victims so that the body would be unmarked. They murdered at least 15 people.

One of Burke and Hare's customers was the Scottish anatomist Robert Knox (1791–1862). Knox was a famous lecturer. His lectures on anatomy were very popular, sometimes attracting over 500 students. Knox was the first to attempt to explain human anatomy by comparing humans to other species. However, when the crimes of Burke and Hare were exposed to the public, the body of their final victim was found in Knox's rooms. Knox fled from Edinburgh to Glasgow in 1829.

William Burke was hanged in 1829 from the evidence given by his partner William Hare. Hare is said to have died on the streets of London, a poor beggar, in the 1860s.

In 1832, the Anatomy Act was passed. This allowed the bodies of poor people who lived in government institutions (called paupers) to be used for dissection if they were not claimed by their families. This removed the need for body snatching. In the UK it was not until the 1940s that it became legal to request bodies for dissection.

Braille

Blind people cannot see but their other senses are extremely well developed. They make use of their other senses, especially touch and hearing.

Blind people can identify many things by feeling them. Their fingertips are very sensitive. They also use their sense of touch to read. A French scientist, Louis Braille (1809–1852), invented a reading system for the blind to use. Each letter of the alphabet is represented by a shape consisting of one to six dots which are embossed or raised on thick paper. Braille is not the only system used by the blind to read. An English scientist, Dr Moon, developed another system. In the Moon system the letters are represented by shapes rather than dots. The shapes are very easy to feel and quick to learn. The disadvantage of this system is that it takes up a great deal of room, and so books written in Moon are very thick and heavy.

Figure 2 *Reading braille*

Questions

1 Who was Leonardo da Vinci? *[Total 1]*

2 What is Vetruvian man? *[Total 1]*

3 How did da Vinci work out the proportions of the body? *[Total 1]*

4 Explain what dissection is. *[Total 2]*

5 Whose bodies could be used for dissections in Britain
   a) before 1832 *[1]*
   b) after 1832? *[1]*
   [Total 2]

6 a) Who were Burke and Hare? *[1]*
   b) How did Burke and Hare get bodies? *[2]*
   [Total 3]

7 Who was Robert Knox? *[Total 1]*

8 Why do blind people need very sensitive finger tips? *[Total 1]*

9 Who was Louis Braille? *[Total 1]*

10 Describe his invention. *[Total 2]*

11 Who was Dr Moon? *[Total 1]*

12 Describe his invention. *[Total 2]*

13 Why do you think that people who go blind when they are young learn Braille, whereas elderly people who go blind tend to learn Moon? *[Total 3]*.

Applications

The bones tell their story

Figure 1

Archaeologists analyse bones and are able to gather information about people who have died. After the adolescent growth spurt, the soft regions at the ends of the long bones become hard, containing calcium phosphate. There is little or no further growth in height. If, during a person's life, there was a time of serious illness or starvation, bone growth stops temporarily, until the illness gets better. This stop in the growth is marked on the bone forever as a pale horizontal line. Archaeologists look at bones closely as this gives information about diet and disease in people who died hundreds of years ago.

The archaeologist can calculate the height of a person by using the length of the femur as a gauge. They can also work out the approximate size of different muscles by studying the joints. Larger muscles leave bigger marks where tendons were joined.

Supermarkets and senses

Large supermarkets are designed carefully. The designers want the customers to stay in the store for as long as possible and they want to encourage the customers to buy as much as possible. The store designers try to stimulate all the senses.

- Melodic music is played in the background. This is not too loud as it would be regarded as a nuisance by many customers. The music is seldom from current pop charts as the store has customers with a range of musical preferences. The music is designed to help relax the customer.
- Low level lighting is used in the main part of the store. Florescent lighting is used for the signs of the different sections within the store such as the bakery. The main lighting is designed to be soothing, without glare.
- Many supermarkets now have in-store bakeries and coffee shops. The aroma from the bakery is piped back into the store. This has the effect of making people feel hungry. They may then buy more than they need or they may stop in the coffee shop for refreshment.
- Samples of products are often available. Tasting the products has the effect of encouraging customers to buy new product.

When collagen (a type of protein found in bones and ligaments) fibres are heated they form glue. Collagen is also used a great deal in the cosmetics industry. It is added to facial moisturisers, to help skin feel smoother.

Uses of plant hormones

Fruits such as bananas produce a chemical called ethene. The ethene helps the fruit to ripen. Unripe bananas are picked in the Caribbean to be shipped to Europe. While the fruits are being transported plant growth substances are sprayed onto them to slow down ripening. Once they arrive in Europe, they are exposed to ethene gas which ripens them.

The hormone giberellin is used to increase stem growth between the places where leaves are attached. This makes the fruit grow bigger and it also helps the seeds to germinate.

Abscisic acid is a hormone which is used to slow down the growth of cells in roots and stems. If this hormone is sprayed on to leaves they will begin to wither and fall.

Gardeners use auxin based hormonal rooting powders to help stimulate root growth of cutting. The cuttings are sections taken from a healthy plant which can be planted. The cuttings develop and grow.

Figure 2 *Bananas are exposed to ethene gas to help ripen them.*

Questions

1 Why is it useful to slow down the ripening process?
[Total 1]

2 What type of hormone is used in plant rooting powder? *[Total 1]*

3 A gardener wants to get a bigger crop of apples this year. What could he do to achieve this? *[Total 1]*

4 Which hormone might be used to clear a wooded area of leaves? *[Total 1]*

5 Design a leaflet to help supermarket managers make their shops attractive to customers. *[Total 4]*

Questions

1 Why is it important that a good diet contains calcium? *[Total 1]*

2 a) Why do muscles work in pairs? *[1]*
b) Explain why muscles pull but do not push. *[2]*
[Total 3]

3 Using the diagram of the skeleton on page 85 match the bones listed with the correct region of the body. *[Total 7]*

Bones:	Regions:
ribs, humerus, tibia, skull,	neck, arm, hips,
pelvis, vertebrae, fibula	leg, head, chest

4 Explain why it is mainly elderly people who undergo hip replacement operations. *[Total 1]*

5 a) Organs (excluding bones and muscles) account for 20 % of the body's weight, muscles account for 45% of the weight. Calculate the mass of your skeleton. *[1]*
b) What percentage of your total body mass is your skeleton? *[2]*
[Total 3]

6 a) Why is it important to be able to detect changes in the environment? *[1]*
b) Name the type of response used when a person lets go of a hot saucepan handle. *[1]*
[Total 2]

7 List three activities that might confuse your sense of balance. *[Total 3]*

8 a) Suggest reasons to explain why the brain is surrounded by bone. *[1]*
b) How is the eye protected? *[3]*
[Total 4]

9 Why is it important that reflex actions are fast? *[Total 1]*

10 a) Why are the three small bones of the ear important? *[2]*
b) What jobs are done by the eardrum, oval window and the fluid in the cochlea? *[3]*
[Total 5]

11 What is a receptor? *[Total 1]*

12 Explain what happens when we hear. *[Total 6]*

13 a) Explain what happens when we see. *[4]*
b) Explain why animals that come out at night have lots of rods in their retina. *[1]*
[Total 5]

14 What do you think the effect of using growth hormone on meat cattle might be? *[Total 1]*

15 Some crops such as rhubarb are grown in dark tubes. Explain why this is done. *[Total 1]*

16 a) Where are hormones made? *[1]*
b) If you were being chased by a dog which hormone would your body be releasing? *[1]*
[Total 2]

17 a) What is insulin? *[1]*
b) What effect does insulin have on the body? *[3]*
[Total 4]

18 Outline the different sensations detected by sensory receptors as you take off your shoes and clothes and get into a hot bath. *[Total 2]*
a) Suggest the effect eating two chocolate bars might have on a diabetic. *[1]*
b) Explain how the body would try to correct the situation. *[1]*
c) What would the diabetic person need to do? *[1]*
[Total 3]

19
R Find out what a physiotherapist does and how they deal with sports injuries.

20
R Find out about different bone fractures and how they are treated.

21
R Find out what effect different drugs have on the nervous system e.g. cannabis, ecstasy, heroin. You could find out about long term and short term effects.

22
R Find out what research was carried out by Dutch scientist, Fritz Went.

23
R Find out about diseases of the nervous system e.g. multiple sclerosis, Parkinson's disease and Altzheimer's.

24
R Try to find out about the role of a physiotherapist and how they deal with sports injuries.

25
P Investigate how sensitive different parts of the body are to stimuli.

26
P Investigate your reaction times. Are your reactions quicker with your left or right hand?

27
P Investigate the effect of light on young seedlings.

28
P Investigate to see if you can detect different flavours when blindfolded.

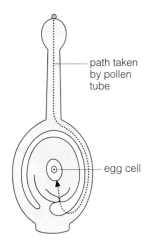

Figure 1.6 *Fertilisation in a plant.*

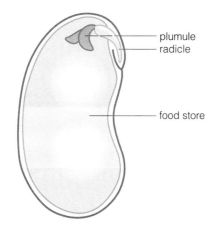

Figure 1.7

Fertilisation

Fertilisation is the fusion of the male sex cell with the female sex cell. Together they produce a single cell that can grow into a new plant. When a pollen grain lands on the ripe stigma, it grows a long **pollen tube** down through the style to the ovary. The male nucleus travels down the tube until it reaches an ovule inside the ovary. The male nucleus from the pollen grain **fertilises** the female sex cell in the ovule.

After fertilisation the ovule develops into a seed which begins to grow. The petals and stamens of the flower fall away. The ovary is left and this swells to form the fruit as the seeds grow.

Seeds and fruit

After fertilisation the fertilised ovule divides into many cells to form a seed. The seed develops a thick tough outer coat for protection. The seed then grows in two parts:

- the embryo – this contains a **plumule** which grows into the shoot and the **radicle** which becomes the root.
- the food store – cells packed with starch or oil. The food store may be part of the embryo.

When the seed germinates, the embryo must have a source of food. The food store in the seed provides nutrients for growth until the seedling photosynthesises and can make its own food. This food store also provides food for many animals. We eat many foods that are seeds, e.g. wheat flour for bread, rice, beans and corn on the cob.

We usually think of fruits in terms of apples and pears, but a complete ovary after fertilisation is a **fruit**. In other words an ovary is a structure packed with fertile seeds. The ovary wall grows and develops as the seed grows. When a fruit is cut open seeds can be seen inside.

Figure 1.8

Dispersal

There is increased chance of survival for new plants if the seeds are scattered or **dispersed** as far as possible from the parent plant. The seed cannot grow and develop in shadow or overcrowded conditions. It is also better for the species if the seedlings start to grow in new places. There are many different ways that seeds and fruits can be dispersed.

- **Wind dispersal.** This happens to plants such as the poppy whose seeds are light and are simply blown and spread by the wind. Sycamore seeds have wings, which allow them to move through the air, far away from the parent. In other plants such as the dandelion, little hairs attached to the ovary help carry the fruits through the air.

Figure 1.9 *Seeds dispersed by the wind.*

- **Animal dispersal.** There are two methods. When fruits are eaten by animals, the seeds in the fruit pass through the animal and are egested in their droppings. Some fruits have hooks that cling to the fur of animals and are dispersed as the animals move around.

Figure 1.10 *These fruits have hooks.*

- **Water dispersal.** This happens to plants which grow near the water. The seeds contain air spaces that help them to float, and they are carried away on currents.

- **Self-dispersal.** This happens when the fruit walls of some plants simply dry out and burst. The split ovary scatters all its seeds explosively.

Figure 1.11 *Water dispersal.*

Figure 1.12 *Self-dispersal.*

Germination

When a seed starts to grow this is called **germination**. Seeds will only germinate if conditions are right. Three conditions are needed for germination: water, warmth and oxygen. As seeds germinate, a radicle (root) grows downward and a plumule (shoot) grows upwards towards the light. Seeds have their own food store but they are quickly used up. Once the plant emerges into the light the leaves of the seedling open out and begin to make chlorophyll. The new plant can then make its own food by photosynthesis.

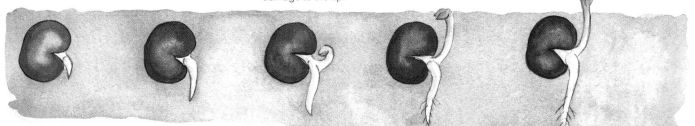

The root starts growing out.

The root grows down into the soil.

The shoot grows out. It is hook-shaped to prevent damage to the tip.

The root continues to grow down and the shoot grows up.

The shoot breaks through the surface of the soil and straightens. The first leaves open out. Side branches grow out from the main root.

Figure 1.13 *Germination of a seed.*

Asexual reproduction

Asexual reproduction is reproduction with only one parent. The offspring produced are genetically identical to their parent. The advantages of asexual reproduction are:

- many offspring can be produced quickly
- favourable conditions are maximised efficiently.

The main disadvantage of asexual reproduction is that the offspring are more likely to be killed by outbreaks of disease. They do not have the genetic variation needed to fight diseases.

Some new plants can be produced without seeds. Asexual reproduction in plants is also called **vegetative reproduction**. There are two main ways that this can happen.

- Bulbs and tubers – these are the swollen roots or stems of plants which if planted grow into new plants. Potatoes are tubers, and onions are bulbs.

Figure 1.14

- Runners – these are side branches of some plants that grow along the surface of the soil. Roots grow down from buds on the runners. These develop into new plants. Strawberry plants reproduce in this way.

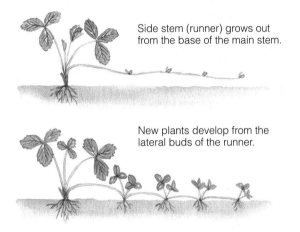

Side stem (runner) grows out from the base of the main stem.

New plants develop from the lateral buds of the runner.

Figure 1.15 *Strawberry runners.*

There are many different ways that plants can be reproduced artificially.

- Cuttings – this method involves cutting a small piece of the stem which has leaves, away from a plant. The cutting is then placed in water until roots develop. The plant is placed in soil and develops into a new plant. To speed up the process hormone rooting powder can be used on the end of the cutting and the cutting can be put straight into the soil.

Figure 1.16 *A plant cutting that has started to develop roots.*

- Grafts – this method involves making a cut into the stem of a tree. A small stem from another tree which has buds is fitted into the cut.

Figure 1.17 *Bitumen is applied to this grafted apple tree to prevent drying out.*

Cloning – this involves taking small pieces of a plant and placing them in a sterile nutrient solution where the cells can multiply. Separate cells are then taken out, placed into different sterile nutrient solutions with plant growth substances and allowed to develop to form many embryos. Each embryo then develops into a new plant. This procedure is also called **tissue culture**.

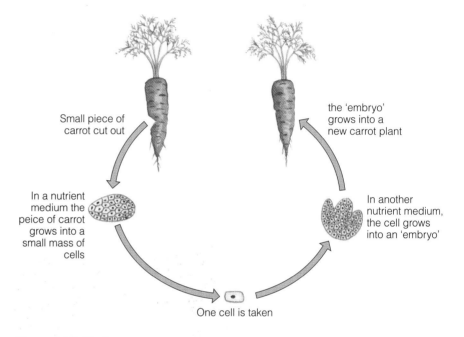

Small piece of carrot cut out

In a nutrient medium the peice of carrot grows into a small mass of cells

One cell is taken

In another nutrient medium, the cell grows into an 'embryo'

the 'embryo' grows into a new carrot plant

Figure 1.18 *Cloning.*

Summary

- Flowering plants reproduce by sexual reproduction.
- Male sex cells are contained in pollen grains and female sex cells are contained in ovules.
- Flowers may be pollinated by insects or wind.
- Pollination is the transfer of pollen from anthers to stigmas.
- Fertilisation involves the fusing together of the male and female sex cells.
- The swollen ovary of a plant becomes a fruit.
- Seeds may be dispersed by wind, water, animals or by the fruit.
- Three conditions are needed for germination: water, warmth and oxygen.
- Asexual reproduction needs only one parent.

Questions

1 Copy and complete the following sentences.
There are four main parts in a flowering plant
_____, _____, _____,
and _____. Sexual _____ is where
a _____ gamete joins with a _____
gamete. The male sex cell is in the _____
and the female sex cell is in the _____.
_____ reproduction requires only
one parent plant. *[Total 5]*

2 a) Which part of the plant prevents it from being
blown over? *[1]*
b) Where is water absorbed in a plant? *[1]*
c) What part of the plant transports water to the
leaves and food to the roots? *[1]*
d) Which part of the plant carries out
photosynthesis? *[1]*
[Total 4]

3 a) What is the function of a flower? *[1]*
b) Explain what gametes are. *[1]*
c) List and give the functions of the female
parts of a flower. *[3]*
d) List and give the functions of the male
parts of a flower. *[2]*
[Total 7]

4 a) What is pollination? *[1]*
b) What are the different types of pollination? *[4]*
c) What is fertilisation? *[1]*
d) Explain the difference between pollination
and fertilisation. *[3]*
[Total 9]

5 a) What do the ovules become after
fertilisation? *[1]*
b) Name the parts of a seed. *[2]*
[Total 3]

6 In an experiment broad beans were grown in jars
(Figure 1.19). The data collected are given in Table 1.1.
a) Draw a graph of this data (include a key). *[6]*
b) Describe what has happened. *[3]*
[Total 9]

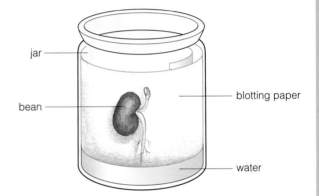

Figure 1.19

Day	Length of radicle (mm)	Length of plumule (mm)	Total length of seedling (mm)
1	0	0	0
2	1	0	1
3	2	0	2
6	3	1	4
18	12	6	18

Table 1.1

7 a) What is dispersal? *[1]*
b) Outline the two possible parts that animals
play in dispersal. *[2]*
[Total 3]

8 Why is it important that seeds grow away from their
parent plant? *[Total 3]*

5.2 Reproduction in animals

How do humans reproduce? Humans reproduce through sexual reproduction. A human fetus develops for nine months in the mother's uterus before being born.

Making cells

There are two ways by which new cells can be made. The first way is called **mitosis**, which happens when organisms are growing or replacing old or damaged cells. This can also happen during asexual reproduction. **Asexual reproduction** is a special type of reproduction that involves only one parent. In some forms of asexual reproduction the organism splits into two. Organisms such as yeast reproduce by dividing into two in this way. This is known as budding. (Yeast is a fungus and not an animal.) Each new cell that is produced is called a daughter cell. The new cells have exactly the same genetic code as the parent.

During mitosis the nucleus of the cell divides, so that the daughter cells have an identical set of genes to the parent cell. Genes are carried in the nucleus on long strands called chromosomes. Nearly all the cells in your body have 46 chromosomes in the nucleus. The new cells formed from mitosis are **clones**, exact replicas of the parent cell.

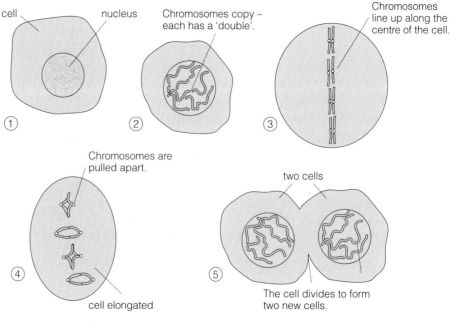

Figure 2.1 *Mitosis*

Meiosis is the other way in which new cells can be made. Meiosis results in gametes having half the number of chromosomes as the parent cell. Meiosis happens in the production of sex cells. Sex cells are called **gametes**. After meiosis, a human sex cell contains 23 chromosomes rather than 46. Fertilisation involves the nucleus of a female sex cell fusing with the nucleus of a male sex cell giving the fertilised egg 46 chromosomes again.

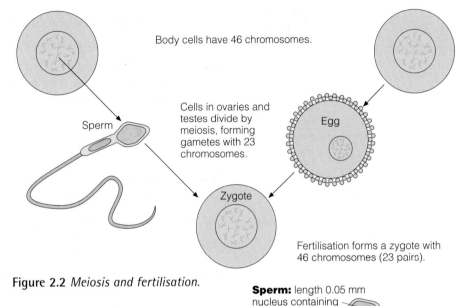

Body cells have 46 chromosomes.

Cells in ovaries and testes divide by meiosis, forming gametes with 23 chromosomes.

Fertilisation forms a zygote with 46 chromosomes (23 pairs).

Figure 2.2 *Meiosis and fertilisation.*

Sex cells

There are two types of sex cell in humans: the female egg cell is called the **ovum**, and the male cell is called the **sperm**. Both of these cells are specially adapted to their functions. The female cell has large food reserves in the cytoplasm and so is big and round. The male cell has a long tail and streamlined body because it needs to swim. The sperm cell also has chemicals called enzymes in the 'head' to help it digest away the membrane of the ovum as it makes its way through. During fertilisation each sex cell has a nucleus containing 23 chromosomes.

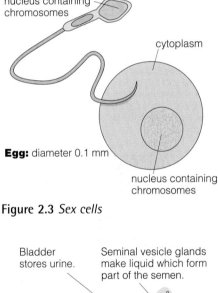

Sperm: length 0.05 mm nucleus containing chromosomes

cytoplasm

Egg: diameter 0.1 mm

nucleus containing chromosomes

Figure 2.3 *Sex cells*

Male reproductive system

Sperm, the male sex cells, are made in the **testes**. The testes hang outside the body in a bag called the **scrotum**. The testes are not inside the body because body temperature is too high for sperm production. Each testis is connected to the **penis** by a tube called the **sperm duct**. Before sperm leave the body they are mixed with a liquid which comes from two small glands called seminal vesicles. Sperm and the liquid are called **semen**. The penis has a tube running through it called the **urethra**. Semen, and urine from the bladder both leave the penis through the urethra. The urethra can carry either semen or urine but not both at the same time.

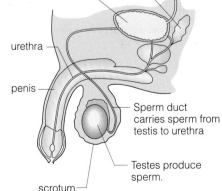

Bladder stores urine.

Seminal vesicle glands make liquid which form part of the semen.

urethra

penis

Sperm duct carries sperm from testis to urethra

Testes produce sperm.

scrotum

Figure 2.4 *Male reproductive system.*

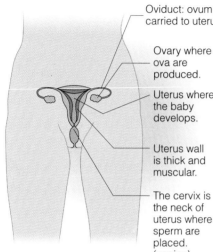

Oviduct: ovum is carried to uterus.

Ovary where ova are produced.

Uterus where the baby develops.

Uterus wall is thick and muscular.

The cervix is the neck of uterus where sperm are placed. (vagina)

Figure 2.5

Female reproductive organs

The ova (egg cells) are made in two **ovaries**. These are found inside the abdomen on either side of the uterus. They are connected to the uterus by tubes called **oviducts**. The ends of the oviducts have funnels, which catch the ova as they are released from the ovaries. An oviduct carries the ovum from the ovary to the **uterus**. The uterus is like a bag with a thick muscular wall where a fertilised egg cell can grow and develop. It takes between four and five days for the ovum to reach the uterus from the ovary. The uterus connects to the outside of the body by a muscular tube called the **vagina**. The neck of the uterus is called the **cervix**.

When a man and woman have sex the penis is inserted into the vagina. Sperm may be released at the neck of the uterus.

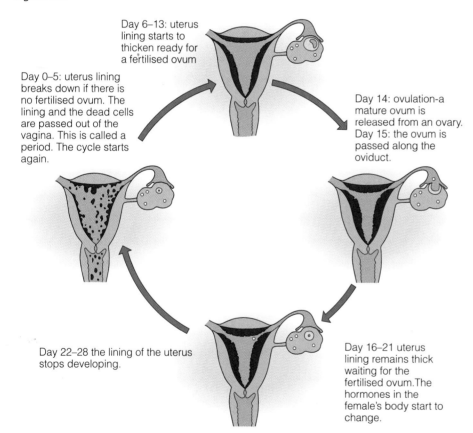

Day 6–13: uterus lining starts to thicken ready for a fertilised ovum

Day 0–5: uterus lining breaks down if there is no fertilised ovum. The lining and the dead cells are passed out of the vagina. This is called a period. The cycle starts again.

Day 14: ovulation-a mature ovum is released from an ovary. Day 15: the ovum is passed along the oviducts.

Day 22–28 the lining of the uterus stops developing.

Day 16–21 uterus lining remains thick waiting for the fertilised ovum. The hormones in the female's body start to change.

Figure 2.6 *Menstrual cycle.*

Menstruation

A girl who has reached puberty releases an ovum from one of her ovaries every 28 days. This is called **ovulation**. Close to the time of ovulation the uterus must prepare itself for the ovum. The lining of the uterus thickens as a network of blood capillaries grows in it. If the ovum is fertilised by a sperm it develops into a baby. If the ovum remains unfertilised, it dies and the lining of the uterus then breaks up. The lining and the dead ovum pass out of the body through the vagina. This is called a **period** or **menstruation**. A period may last between three and seven days. Women use sanitary protection to absorb the blood which is lost.

The menstrual cycle can vary in lengths of time for different women. It can also be painful for some females because the muscles in the uterus wall contract. This may result in cramps and cause stomach and back pains. Occasionally water collects in body tissues which makes them swell up, resulting in swelling of the ankles and fingers.

After menstruation the uterus grows a fresh lining for each new ovum. The cycle of making a new lining and a new ovum is called the **menstrual cycle**. If an ovum is fertilised on day 14 then the lining of the uterus remains, and the placenta develops, partly from the fertilised egg and partly from the mother, to feed and protect the developing embryo. The lining of the womb does not break down this time.

Fertilisation

Sexual intercourse involves a man inserting his penis into the woman's vagina. Before this can be done blood pressure in the tissue stiffens the penis. This is called an **erection**. It happens whenever a man becomes sexually aroused. Once the penis is inside the vagina, sperm may be released. The release of sperm is called **ejaculation**. The sperm are mixed with a small amount of fluid and are squeezed along the sperm duct into the urethra. They are released as semen out of the end of the penis and deposited at the neck of the uterus, the cervix. From here the sperm swim through the uterus and up into the oviducts. This takes about 48 hours. Once in the oviduct they may meet an ovum. Only one sperm can fertilise the ovum.

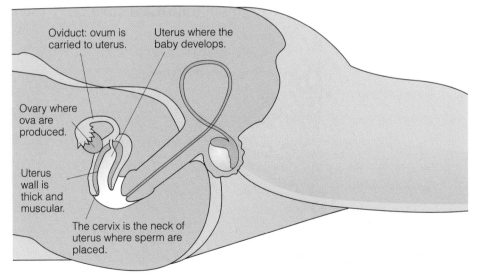

Oviduct: ovum is carried to uterus.

Uterus where the baby develops.

Ovary where ova are produced.

Uterus wall is thick and muscular.

The cervix is the neck of uterus where sperm are placed.

Figure 2.7 *Sexual intercourse.*

Ova (plural of ovum) are much larger than sperm. More than 300 million sperm enter a female during sexual intercourse. Approximately 100 of them reach the ovum but only one occasionally gets in.

When one sperm enters the ovum the surface membranes of the ovum change to stop any more sperm getting into it. After the sperm enters the ovum, the nucleus of the sperm (which contains genetic material) fuses with the nucleus of the ovum. The fusion of the two gametes is called **fertilisation**. A fertilised ovum contains two sets of genetic material. One set comes from each parent so that the new individual will have characteristics from both of the parents and will be unique.

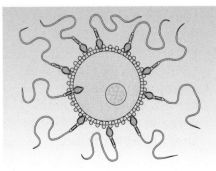

Figure 2.8 *Sperm grouped around an ovum.*

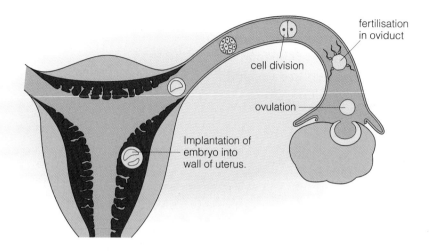

Figure 2.9 *The journey of the ball of cells to the uterus.*

Pregnancy

The newly fertilised ovum then begins to divide by mitosis and moves down the oviduct. Once it reaches the uterus it is a ball of cells. The ball of cells implants itself in the walls of the uterus. It is here that the embryo begins to develop into a baby and the woman is now said to be **pregnant**. For the first two months the ball of cells is called an **embryo**.

After six weeks the embryo has a beating heart and a brain. It is about 1 cm long. The tiny embryo floats in a sac filled with watery liquid called **amniotic fluid** that protects it. The embryo cannot eat or breathe and so a link is formed between the embryo and the uterus to supply food and oxygen. The link is an organ called the **placenta**. The embryo is attached to the placenta by an **umbilical cord**.

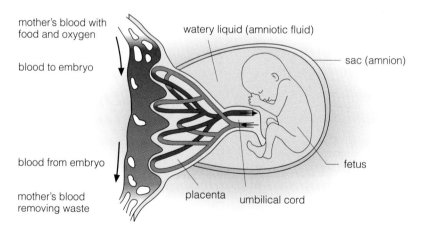

Figure 2.10 *Embryo and placenta.*

The placenta has a large network of capillaries. Food and oxygen diffuse from the mother's blood into the baby's. Waste products like carbon dioxide diffuse from the baby's blood into the mother's. The two blood supplies do not mix. The placenta acts as a barrier to some harmful substances. However some substances like the chemicals in cigarette smoke, alcohol and drugs can cross the placenta and harm the baby.

After about two months the embryo has a head and torso and develops visible limbs. It is now called a **fetus**.

! Girls are given a rubella vaccine when they are about 11 to stop them from catching the disease rubella (German measles). If a woman catches rubella during the first 12 weeks of pregnancy, it can cause deafness, blindness and heart disease in the baby but does not greatly affect the mother.

Development of the fetus

The development of the fetus is shown in Figure 2.11. Some of the main stages are:

- 6 weeks: embryo 1 cm long, umbilical cord forming
- 7 weeks: embryo 2.5 cm long, limbs starting to form
- 3 months: 7 cm long, body almost completely formed
- 6 months: 28 cm long, baby is moving around and kicking, will continue to grow until birth
- 9 months: 50 cm long, fully developed and ready to be born.

Birth

Birth happens approximately nine months after fertilisation. A few days before birth the baby usually turns round so that its head is near the cervix and can emerge first.

As the moment of birth approaches:

- the muscles in the uterus contract strongly (contractions)
- the muscles in the cervix relax
- the bag of fluid around the baby bursts
- the cervix widens
- strong contractions push the baby out through the vagina.

After birth, the baby's umbilical cord is cut to separate it from the placenta. The stub forms the navel or belly button. Shortly after that the muscles in the uterus contract again and push the placenta out. This is sometimes called the afterbirth.

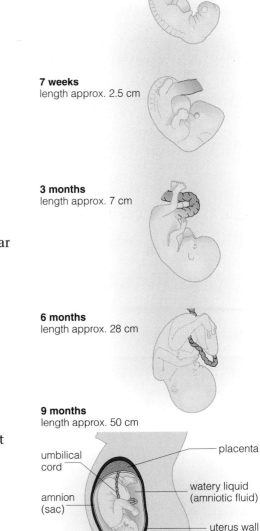

6 weeks
lenght approx. 1 cm

7 weeks
length approx. 2.5 cm

3 months
length approx. 7 cm

6 months
length approx. 28 cm

9 months
length approx. 50 cm

umbilical cord — placenta

amnion (sac) — watery liquid (amniotic fluid)

uterus wall

cervix —

vagina —

Figure 2.11 *Development in the uterus.*

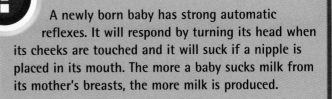

A newly born baby has strong automatic reflexes. It will respond by turning its head when its cheeks are touched and it will suck if a nipple is placed in its mouth. The more a baby sucks milk from its mother's breasts, the more milk is produced.

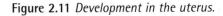

Figure 2.12 *New born baby with umbilical cord.*

Twins

Twins may be formed in one of two ways.

- Sometimes a woman's ovaries release two or more ova at the same time. If they all become fertilised they all develop into babies. Twins formed in this way are non-identical. They develop from different ova fertilised by different sperm.
- Sometimes, after fertilisation, the fertilised ovum splits and divides into two balls of cells. Twins formed in this way are identical. They develop from the same ovum.

Identical twins have exactly the same physical characteristics such as the colour of their eyes, hair and skin, shape of their nose, attached ear lobes, blood group and gender. These characteristics are called **inherited characteristics** as they depend on information inherited from parents. Characteristics such as skill at sport and ability to speak a language result from environmental effects and may be different for the twins. Some characteristics, such as height, are the result of a combination of both inheritance and environment.

Summary

- Cells can be made by mitosis or meiosis
- The female sex cell is called the ovum and is made in an ovary.
- The male sex cell is called the sperm and is made in a testis.
- Menstruation is the breaking down of the uterus lining.
- Sexual intercourse allows ovum and sperm to meet in the woman's body.
- Fertilisation is the point when the sperm enters the ovum and the two nuclei fuse, combining genetic material.
- A fertilised ovum grows into a baby inside the uterus
- The fetus is protected by the amniotic fluid and the walls of the uterus.
- The umbilical cord supplies the fetus with oxygen and nutrients and takes away carbon dioxide and urea.

Questions

1 Copy and complete the following sentences. The male reproductive cell is the _____, the female reproductive cell is the _____. An _____ is produced once a month in a cycle called the _____ cycle. If the ovum is not fertilised, then it and the _____ of the uterus are passed out of the _____. This is called a _____. _____ is where a man and woman come together so that the _____ can swim to the _____ and fertilise it. *[Total 5]*

2 List the different ways by which cells can multiply. *[Total 2]*

3 What is asexual reproduction? *[Total 1]*

4 What are clones? *[Total 1]*

5 What is meiosis? *[Total 1]*

6 a) Where are sperm produced? *[1]*
   b) What is semen? *[1]*
   [Total 2]

7 When does a penis become erect? *[Total 1]*

8 a) Where are ova made? *[1]*
   b) What is ovulation? *[1]*
   c) How often is an ovum released? *[1]*
   [Total 3]

9 a) Describe the uterus. *[2]*
   b) Explain what menstruation is. *[2]*
   c) Briefly outline the menstrual cycle. *[5]*
   [Total 9]

10 a) Explain what fertilisation is. *[2]*
   b) At which point is a woman pregnant? *[1]*
   [Total 3]

11 a) Explain the function of the placenta. *[2]*
   b) Describe the difference between an embryo and a fetus. *[2]*
   [Total 4]

12 Using the information in Figure 2.11, draw a graph to show the rate of growth of a fetus. *[Total 6]*

13 When is a fetus ready to be born? *[Total 1]*

14 Explain how identical and non-identical twins are formed. *[Total 4]*

5.3 Human development

What is puberty? Babies are born with reproductive organs but they do not function until puberty. **Puberty** is the time when the reproductive organs become mature.

Puberty

This is the time between childhood and adulthood. A set of physical changes happen during puberty. For girls these changes start between the ages of 11 and 15, and for boys the changes start between the ages of 13 and 15.

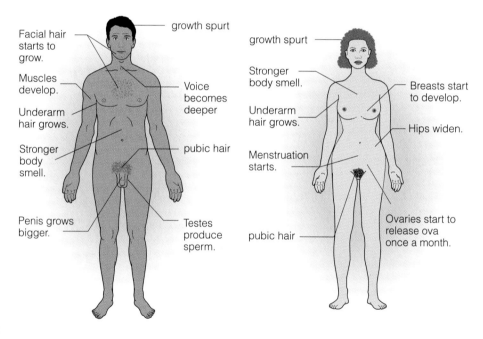

Figure 3.1 *Changes during puberty.*

The physical changes that are produced at puberty are called secondary sexual **characteristics**. They are necessary as individuals enter into the reproductive stage of their lives. Sex hormones control these changes. The main female hormone is called **oestrogen**. The main male hormone is called **testosterone**.

The physical changes are accompanied by emotional changes. Young people, at this stage of development are called **adolescents**. They become sexually mature and more independent from their parents. During puberty adolescents often become self-conscious about the changes in their bodies. They may suffer from mood swings and become irritable. Hormones also make these emotional changes happen.

Birth control

Sexual reproduction is an important part of a loving relationship. Couples who love each other often plan when they are to begin their family. In order to prevent conception or fertilisation they may use birth control measures. There are different methods of birth control which are commonly called **contraceptives**.

Contraceptives can be classified into one of three groups:

- barrier methods – these stop the sperm from reaching the ovum
- chemical methods – these stop the production of ova
- intrauterine (IUD) – these stop the implantation of the fertilised ovum.

Contraceptive	Group	Description	Example
condom	barrier	A thin rubber cover that is placed over an erect penis. The condom is coated with a spermicide. A spermicide is gel which contains chemicals that kill sperm (95% reliable).	
diaphragm	barrier	A dome shaped rubber cover placed over the woman's cervix. Used with a spermicide (96% reliable).	
rhythm method	natural	Couple study the woman's menstrual cycle and avoid having sex near the time of ovulation (75% reliable).	
morning after pill (emergency contraception)	chemical	Two pills are taken by the female within 72 hours of sexual intercourse. The dose of two pills is repeated 12 hours later. The pills contain hormones which stop implantation taking place (99% reliable).	
pill	chemical	A pill is swallowed by the woman every day for 21 days of the 28-day cycle. The pill contains hormones which stop the ovaries releasing ova (98% reliable).	
coil	IUD	A plastic coil is fitted into the uterus. This stops the ball of cells implanting into the lining of the uterus (97% reliable).	

Table 3.1 *Examples of contraceptives.*

The History of Childbirth and Contraception

There have been many changes in attitude to contraception, pregnancy and childbirth. At one time these were not respectable issues to study, but as society has changed it has become more acceptable for scientists and doctors to investigate these areas.

Pregnancy and Childbirth

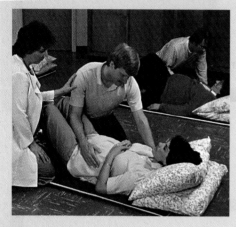

Figure 1

Doctors and well-trained midwives are usually involved at every stage of a woman's pregnancy, and at the birth of her child. However, this wasn't always the case. Before the 18th century, doctors had hardly any contact with women who were pregnant or giving birth. Women did not receive any of the help and advice which is common today.

During a birth the local midwife attended to the mother, usually helped out by friends. The midwife usually had little training. The only time a doctor might be called was if the labour had lasted too long (on average after three days!). The doctor would be called to remove the child who was probably stillborn (born dead), and to save the mother's life. As a result women did not want to call a doctor because the arrival of the doctor was associated with the death of the baby.

In the 18th century an English family, the Chamberlans, started to educate people in the use of forceps. Forceps were used to grip the child's head to help its movement along the birth canal. They were mainly used when the shape of a woman's body caused difficulties during birth. The Chamberlan family proved that using forceps meant a much greater survival rate for mothers and their babies.

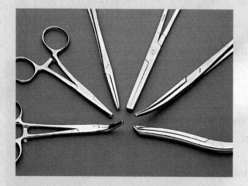

Figure 2 *An assortment of forceps.*

These developments changed the attitude of women towards doctors. When it was seen that doctors might be able to save a child, women became less afraid of calling them. As doctors became more involved they were able to see more births and learn about the whole process.

Birth Control and Hormones

The two most commonly used contraceptive methods today are the Pill and the sheath (condom). The Pill was developed in the 1950s and women in America and England began using it in the 1960s. However, contraceptives have been in use for a very long time in one form or another.

Condoms are not as modern as you might think. One of the earliest uses was recorded in 1564. A man called Gabriello Fallopio wrote about the use of a small linen covering which could protect the glands from infection. The sheaths were made of animal bladders or fine skins.

In the 18th and 19th centuries contraception was a delicate issue. In Britain, as in many other countries, the government and the Church were both opposed to the use of contraception. This was because it was seen as an immoral way of interfering in God's work. However, contraception was a necessity for many couples, especially if the family had several children already. Many couples could not afford to keep having more children.

It was not until the invention of the Pill that birth control was considered to be part of a doctor's education and a suitable subject for scientific investigation. The invention of the Pill is strongly connected to the discovery of the sex hormones. Sex hormones were discovered in the 1920s, and were thought to define the difference between a man and a woman. Sex hormones like testosterone and oestrogen play a major role in sexual development.

In 1921 the scientist Ludwig Haberlandt transferred the ovaries of pregnant rabbits (a source of the female sex hormone) into animals that were not pregnant. The effect was to make the animal temporarily sterile. Haberlandt did not follow up this discovery and it took thirty years before the research was resumed.

In the early 1950s the American health campaigner Margaret Sanger asked a scientist, Gregory Pincus, to try and develop the idea of using sex hormones to stop egg cells being produced. This eventually lead to the development of a contraceptive pill. Once scientists began to work on the problem they developed the Pill quite quickly. It was tested first on animals, and the first women to use it lived in Puerto Rico. As more and more woman used this highly reliable method, it became more acceptable in society. Since they were one of the few people that could actually prescribe the Pill, doctors could now see contraception as a medical matter and became more involved in all aspects of contraception.

Questions

1 What were women's opinions about doctors involved in childbirth before the 18th century? *[Total 1]*

2 How and why did their attitudes change? *[Total 3]*

3 Why was it important for couples to control the number of children that they had? *[Total 2]*

4 When was it first discovered that sex hormones could be used to control fertility? *[Total 1]*

5 a) When did scientists begin to use this information to develop a contraceptive for humans? *[1]*
   b) Who developed the Pill *[1]*
   [Total 2]

Applications

Cloning

Cloning is widely used by gardeners and horticulturists. A carrot was first cloned by Frederick Steward in the 1950s from a single carrot cell. Cloning of plants is fairly easy to carry out and is now commonplace. Fruit trees, such as those which produce Bramley apples, and plants, such as orchids, are almost always produced commercially by cloning.

Cloning of animals is more complex, but in 1996 a sheep was cloned (see Section 7, Applications).

Medical uses of hormones

We know that the menstrual cycle is controlled by hormones. Hormones have a strong effect on the female body. The main female hormones are oestrogen and progesterone. Oestrogen causes the lining of the uterus to thicken so that a fertilised ovum can implant onto the wall and develop into an embryo. Progesterone maintains the uterus wall, and can also block other chemicals that occur in the body. When fertilisation occurs the placenta develops and produces progesterone. As long as progesterone levels stay high the lining of the womb will not breakdown. Tests based on measuring hormone levels are used to detect pregnancy.

If a woman does not wish to become pregnant she can take a contraceptive pill. Contraceptive pills can prevent ovulation. They contain oestrogen and/or progesterone. Hormonal contraceptives can also be implanted under the skin.

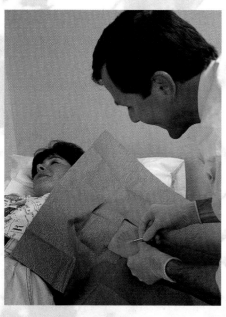

Figure 1 *Implanting contraceptive hormones under the skin.*

Women who want to have a baby but are finding it difficult can have a hormone based treatment to help them. Some women can take drugs called clomiphene which block the effects of the hormone oestrogen and leads to super-ovulation. This means that lots of egg cells are released from the ovaries. Some women are given clomiphene so that their ova can be collected and fertilised outside the body and then put back. This treatment is called IVF (*in vitro* fertilisation).

Figure 2 *Louise Brown, the first IVF baby.*

When a woman gets to about fifty, hormone levels in her body begin to alter. This time of life is called the menopause. Menstruation stops. Oestrogen levels fall. This may cause hot flushes and other problems. Women can be given extra oestrogen through hormone replacement therapy (HRT) at this time. This can be in the form of a patch worn on the body or taken in tablet form.

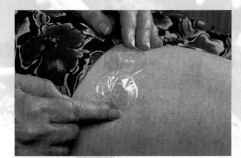

Figure 3 *HRT patches.*

IVF

Occasionally couples find it difficult to conceive. This may be because either the man or the woman is infertile. Infertility can be caused by a number of factors:

- the male has too few sperm to fertilise the ovum
- the female's oviducts may be blocked
- the female's ovaries may not be releasing ova.

There are a variety of treatments that couples who want a baby can try. One method is called *in vitro* fertilisation (IVF). IVF involves ova being taken from the ovaries by keyhole surgery. The ova are fertilised by the sperm in a dish. They are then incubated for 2–3 days. The fertilised ova then divide and form embryos. The stronger embryos are placed into the uterus and the pregnancy continues in the normal way. IVF is not always successful – about 30% of women treated succeed in giving birth. Women who have undergone IVF treatment sometimes have multiple births, because more than one embryo is implanted at once.

Questions

1 What are the main female hormones? [Total 2]

2 a) What produces progesterone after fertilisation? [1]
b) Why is this important? [1]
[Total 2]

3 Explain how hormones can help prevent a woman from becoming pregnant. [Total 4]

4 a) What is clomiphene? [1]
b) What is it used for? [2]
[Total 3]

5 a) Why does the menopause happen? [1]
b) What is HRT? [1]
[Total 2]

6 a) What does infertile mean? [1]
b) List two possible reasons for infertility. [2]
[Total 3]

7 a) How is IVF carried out? [3]
b) Why do some women who have IVF treatment have more than one baby? [1]
[Total 4]

6 Variation and inheritance

6.1 Classification and keys

Why are supermarkets set out in an organised way? Items which are similar are located near to each other. This makes it easier to find the items that we want and compare them. Scientists also arrange organisms into groups. The organisms in a group will have similar features and this makes it easier for scientists to study and compare them. The name of the group also gives us information about the organisms in the group.

Classification

There are millions of types of organisms on the planet. Scientists arrange them into groups based on how similar they are. The largest groups are called kingdoms. All organisms belong to one of the five kingdoms. The kingdoms are:

- **animal** – this group can most simply be subdivided into those with a backbone called **vertebrates** and those without a backbone called **invertebrates**.
- **plant** – further divided into those which produce seeds and those which are seedless, e.g. a fern.
- **fungi** – these include moulds, mushrooms and yeast.
- **protoctista** – these are a wide variety of organisms, some are very simple and have only one cell.
- **prokaryote** – these are single celled organisms with no nucleus and include bacteria and blue-green bacteria.

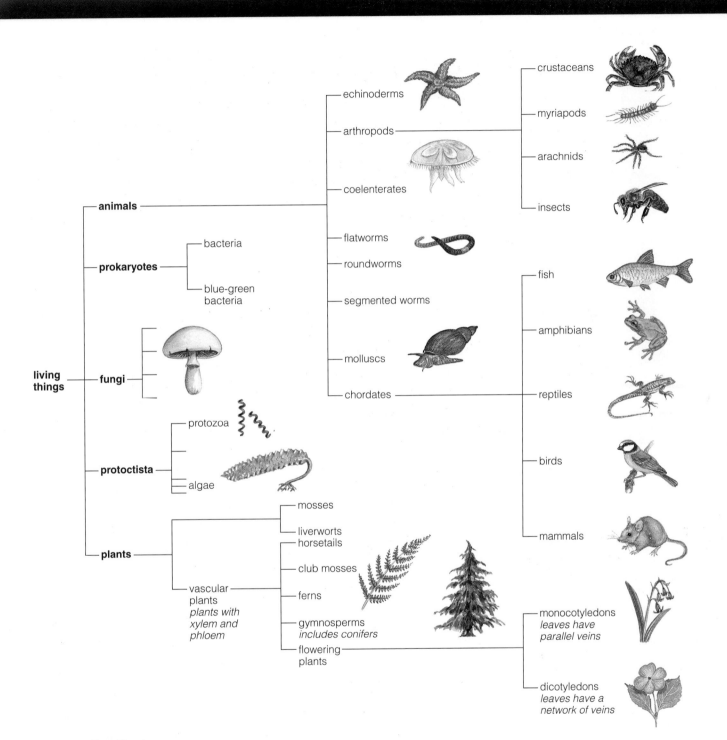

Figure 1.1 *Classification*

Kingdoms can be divided into smaller groups called **phyla**. These can then be subdivided into smaller groups called **classes**. Classes are divided into **orders**, orders into **families**, and families into **genera** (singular genus). Eventually you get to the smallest group called a species.

	Human	Honeybee	Corn	Mushroom
kingdom	Animalia	Animalia	Plantae	Fungi
phylum	Chordata	Arthropoda	Angiospermophyta	Basidiomycota
class	Mammalia	Insecta	Monocotyledoneae	Basidiomycetes
order	Primates	Hymenoptera	Commelinales	Agaricales
family	Hominidae	Apidae	Poaceae	Agaricaceae
genus	*Homo*	*Apis*	*Zea*	*Agaris*
species	*sapiens*	*mellifera*	*mays*	*campestris*

Table 1.1 *Hierarchy of groups.*

! Horses and donkeys can mate and produce a mule but mules are not fertile. So horses and donkeys do not belong to the same species.

Species

The smallest group in the classification of organisms is **species**. A species is a group of organisms that are so alike that they can mate together and produce fertile young.

Humans, horses and dandelions are examples of different species. Members of one species cannot naturally mate with members of another, for example cats cannot mate with dogs.

Animal kingdom

The animal kingdom contains organisms that are very complex. They are made of lots of cells (they are **multicellular**). The animal kingdom can be subdivided into smaller groups called phyla. We belong to a phylum called *chordata*. Nearly all the animals within this phylum are vertebrates. This means that they have backbones. The rest of the phyla in the animal kingdom are known as invertebrates because they do not have a backbone.

Animals with backbones can be placed in one of five classes, as shown in Table 1.2.

Vertebrate class	Characteristics	Examples	Picture
fish	○ streamlined shape ○ breathe through gills ○ move using fins ○ skin has scales ○ live in water ○ eggs laid in water	shark, haddock, salmon, sea horse	
amphibians	○ can live under water breathing through skin ○ adults can live on land as they have lungs ○ moist soft skin ○ eggs laid in water	frog, toad, newt, salamander	
reptiles	○ dry scaly skin ○ lungs ○ eggs with a leathery shell laid on land	tortoise, crocodile, snake	
birds	○ lungs ○ warm blooded ○ feathers ○ eggs with hard shells laid	eagle, sparrow, penguin, owl	
mammals	○ warm blooded ○ young develop inside the mother ○ young feed on milk from the mother ○ lungs ○ fur or hair	bat, human, horse	

Table 1.2 *Vertebrate classification.*

The invertebrates can be subdivided into groups called phyla, as shown in Table 1.3.

Table 1.3 *Invertebrate classification.*

Invertebrate phyla	Characteristic	Examples	Picture
coelenterates	two layered organism with bodies like a bag	jellyfish, hydra, sea anemone	
platyhelminthes	flat bodies	planarian, tapeworm, liver fluke	
annelids	segmented bodies	earthworm, leech	
molluscs	soft bodies protected by one or two shells	snail, limpet, mussels, cuttlefish	
echinoderms	armour plated skins covered in spines	starfish, sea cucumber, sea urchin	
arthropods	animals with hard outer skeleton, segmented bodies and jointed walking limbs	crabs, ticks, beetles ladybirds	

Molluscs only have one foot, echinoderms literally have hundreds.

There are more species of arthropod than any other type of animal. Arthropods can be subdivided into four classes, as shown in Table 1.4.

Arthropod class	Characteristic	Examples	Picture
insects	animals with three pairs of legs and with bodies divided into three parts	grasshopper, dragonfly, stag beetle	
arachnids	animals with four pairs of legs, no antennae, and bodies divided into two parts	spider, scorpion, harvestman	
crustaceans	animals with two pairs of antennae, many legs and hard chalky shells	crabs, lobster, water flea	
myriapods	animals with long thin segmented bodies and many pairs of legs	centipede, millipede	

Table 1.4 *Arthropod classification.*

Plant kingdom

Plants are multicellular organisms. These organisms all contain **chlorophyll**. Chlorophyll is a green chemical, which absorbs light energy. The light energy can be used to make food for the plants. Plants can be roughly divided into smaller groups: those that produce seeds and those that do not.

The seedless plants include:

- Mosses and liverworts. These have no true roots, stems or leaves. They are very small and reproduce by spores. A spore is a reproductive cell that has a thick wall around it.
- Ferns, club mosses and horsetails. They have roots, stems and leaves and reproduce by spores.

The seed producing plants include:

- Conifers, which reproduce using cones. The cones have seeds in them. They have no true flowers and have needle-like leaves.
- Flowering plants which bear flowers. The flowers then turn into fruit which contain seeds.

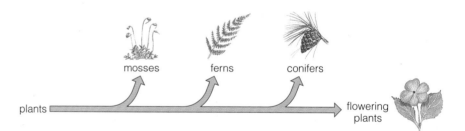

Figure 1.2 *Plant kingdom subdivision.*

Fungi

These were once in the same group as plants but are now a separate group. They do not contain chlorophyll and cannot photosynthesise. Most fungi are multicellular. Yeast is the exception as it is **unicellular**. Uniellular organisms are made of one cell.

Fungi are usually made up of fine branched threads called **hyphae**. The hyphae spread out in a network called a **mycelium**, like bread mould. When the mycelium reaches a certain size it forms reproductive structures which contain spores. Some fungi such as mushrooms produce large structures called fruiting bodies. These are bundles of hyphae joined together. The fruiting body is in two parts: the stalk and the cap. The cap contains gills which produce spores.

Figure 1.3 *Bread mould and mushrooms.*

Most fungi are decomposers called **saprobionts**. They feed on dead matter, decomposing it. A few may feed as parasites in living tissues and can cause diseases such as ringworm in humans.

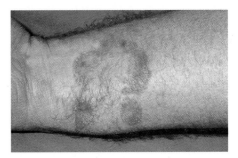
Figure 1.4 *A person with ringworm.*

Protoctista

Protoctista live in water and damp places. Some are unicellular and all have a nucleus in each cell. The unicellular protocista have developed rather special ways to move their bodies. Some move by making the contents of their cell flow. Many, like the *Amoeba*, push out parts of their cells to form temporary arm-like projections called **pseudopodia**. The pseudopodia are then used to catch food, which is usually other protoctista or bacteria.

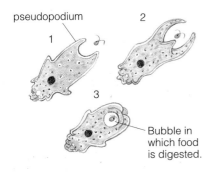

pseudopodium
1
2
3
Bubble in which food is digested.

Figure 1.5 *An amoeba.*

Some, like the *Euglena*, have chlorophyll and so gain energy from photosynthesis. However they move in a different way to amoeba. *Euglena* have a long hair – like projection called a **flagellum**. They move by lashing the flagellum like a whip to propel themselves forward through water.

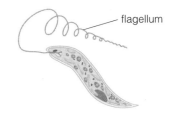
flagellum

Figure 1.6 *Euglena.*

Other protoctista such as *Paramecium* have tiny hairs called cilia over the surface of their bodies. They flick the cilia backwards and forward in a wave-like motion, to push their bodies through the water. The currents of water they generate also suck food into their mouths.

The protoctista kingdom also contains algae such as seaweeds.

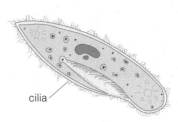
cilia

Figure 1.7 *Paramecium.*

Prokaryotes

These organisms are single celled (unicellular). Their cells do not have a nucleus. All of their genetic material is free in the cytoplasm of the cell. This group can be subdivided into two smaller groups: bacteria and blue-green bacteria.

- **Bacteria** – most are decomposers. They can be classified according to their shape: rounded, coiled or rod shaped. They may be able to live on ther own but may cause serious diseases, e.g. cholera. The ones which cause serious diseases are usually parasitic.

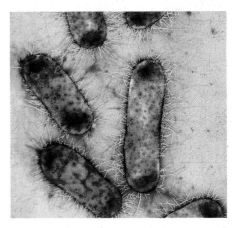
Figure 1.8

> **!** Viruses are considered to be non-living and are not included in the biological classification system.

● **Blue-green bacteria**
– these gain energy from photosynthesis in seas, oceans and damp places on land. They occur in many forms, as single cells, jelly like clusters, or fine threads called filaments. Sometimes they multiply rapidly when the weather is warm to form 'blooms'. They may release poisonous substances into water, which kills animals.

Figure 1.9 *Algal bloom.*

> **!** 400 000 species of beetle and 8000 species of mammal had been identified by 1951. The naturalist, David Attenborough, once said, 'The Creator, if He exists, has a special preference for beetles.' There are about three times as many species of insects as all other kinds of animals put together.

Identifying organisms

More than 1 500 000 different types of organism have been found and identified. Every day more are discovered. Individual scientists cannot remember the names of every organism. When they want to find out which species an organism belongs to or its name, they use a device called a **key**. A key is a special chart, which consists of descriptions and information that make identifying organisms easier.

There are different types of keys. The simplest types are in the form of numbered questions with two possible alternative answers. The answer for each question leads on to another question or the name of the organism. Eventually the name of the unknown organism is found.

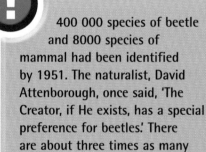

Key		
Question		If yes:
1 Hind legs pointed and hairy?	→	diving beetle (A)
All legs with two claws?	→	2
2 Wing cases small?	→	rove beetle (B)
Wing cases large?	→	3
3 Large jaws?	→	stag beetle (F)
Small jaws?	→	4
4 Antennae have hairs on tip?	→	cockchafer (C)
No hairs on antennae?	→	5
5 Antennae longer than body?	→	long-horned beetle (D)
Antennae shorter than body?	→	weevil (E)

A   B   C   D   E   F

Figure 1.10 *Identifying beetles using a key (not to scale).*

To use the key you must look at the drawings carefully. Read the first pair of questions. Decide which description fits, and if the arrow does not point to a name it will point to another question. That is the next question to read and then work your way through the key until the organism has a name.

Another type of key is the branching or spider key. As you read each question you are given a choice of two branches to follow. You need to follow the route which is the best match until the organism has a name. You still need to look at the drawings carefully.

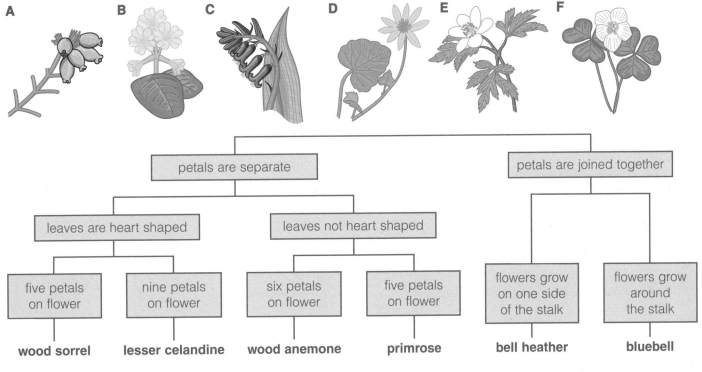

Figure 1.11 *Branching key to identify some wild flowers.*

Summary

- Organisms can be classified into groups according to their main characteristics.
- The groups are kingdom, phylum, class, order, family, genus and species.
- There are five different kingdoms: plant, animal, fungi, protoctista and prokaryote.
- A key can be used in the identification of a living thing.

Questions

1 Copy and complete the following sentences. All living things can be _____ into groups. The _____ major divisions are called _____. The two major divisions of the animal kingdom are _____ and _____. A _____ can help you identify and name an organism. *[Total 3]*

2 a) What does classification mean? *[1]*
   b) What do scientists look for when classifying organisms? *[1]*
   c) In classification, what is a kingdom? *[1]*
   [Total 3]

3 What determines if an animal is called a vertebrate or an invertebrate? *[Total 1]*

4 Explain what a species is. *[Total 3]*

5 Which group of animals have wings and six legs? *[Total 1]*

6 What class of animal is a snake? *[Total 1]*

7 a) Which animals can breathe on land and in water? *[1]*
   b) Explain how they are able to do this. *[2]*
   [Total 3]

8 A reptile and an amphibian both lay eggs. Describe how they are different. *[Total 2]*

9 Which types of sea animals have armour plated bodies? *[Total 1]*

10 What is chlorophyll and which kingdom contains it? *[Total 2]*

11 What are spores and where are they found? *[Total 3]*

12 Explain the differences between mosses and conifers. *[Total 3]*

13 Why are fungi in a different group to plants? *[Total 1]*

14 List a difference and a similarity between prokaryotes and protoctista *[Total 2]*

15 What are pseudopodia, flagellum and cilia used for? *[Total 1]*

16 Explain why a botanist (plant biologist) might use a key. *[Total 1]*

17 Make a branched key for the six shapes in Figure 1.12. *[Total 3]*

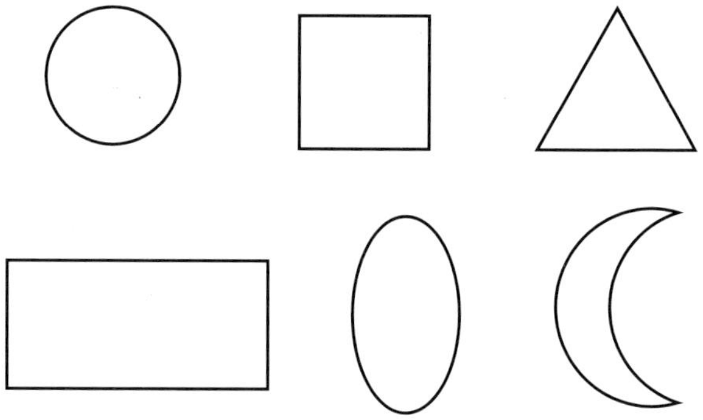

Figure 1.12

18 Make a numbered key for the four pond animals in the diagram. *[Total 3]*

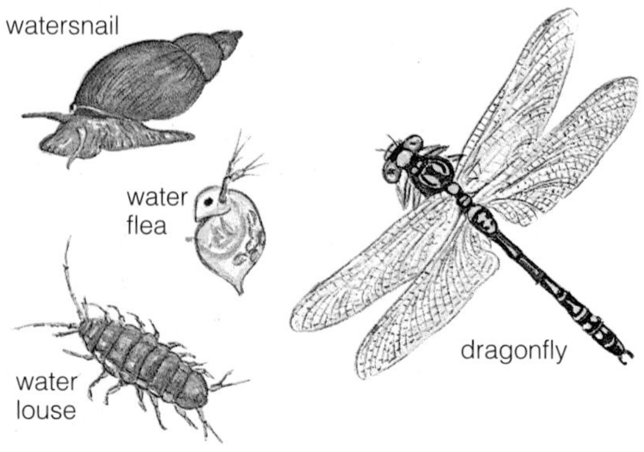

watersnail
water flea
dragonfly
water louse

Figure 1.13

6.2 Why do organisms vary?

Why do we all look different? Humans have different features, such as eye colour, hair colour or blood groups. These are called **characteristics**. The characteristics of all humans are similar because we belong to the same species, *Homo sapiens*. Members of one species live in similar ways, move in similar ways, need similar food and can breed together to produce fertile offspring.

The differences we find between members of the same species are called **variation**.

Types of variation

There are two types of variation: **continuous** and **discontinuous**.

If you measured the heights of all the pupils in your class, some would be shorter, some tall and some in-between. This type of variation is called **continuous variation**, as the characteristic (height) varies in small amounts between individuals from the shortest to the tallest.

Figure 2.1

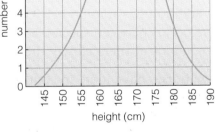

Figure 2.2 *Average heights.*

When we collect data about continuous variation we can show the information using a line graph. This is called the *normal distribution*.

If you asked all the people in your class to roll their tongues some would be able to do it and the others would not. There would be no one in-between. This type of variation is called **discontinuous variation**. Other examples of discontinuous variation include the attachment of ear lobes (are they attached or not?), blood groupings and inherited genetic diseases such as cystic fibrosis. When we collect data of discontinuous variation we show the information in bar charts.

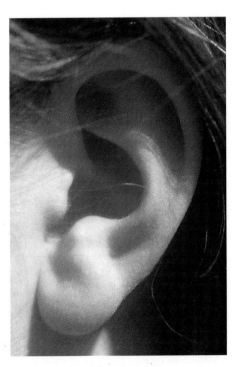

Figure 2.3 *Ear lobes are examples of discontinuous variation.*

139

Causes of variation

Most of the characteristics that you have are passed on to you from your parents, through genes. Genes are small sections of DNA which control a particular characteristic. Genes control the colour of your eyes. Within a family there may be variation in eye colour. This type of variation is caused by the genes or **genetic factors**. There are many other characteristics which are inherited in this way.

Figure 2.4

Figure 2.5 *Identical twins with variation caused by environmental factors.*

Some characteristics are due to factors around us, for example how much food we eat. Diet can affect height, weight and other features. This type of variation is caused by **environmental factors**. Characteristics depend partly on genetic factors and partly on environmental factors. This is so for most organisms, e.g. two trees may have the same genes. However, one may grow better than the other because it receives a better supply of water or more light.

Variation between species

In addition to variation between individuals within a species, variation also occurs between species. Some organisms look the same at first. If you look at them closely there are differences between them.

Two horses have more in common with each other than a horse with a monkey. However, some species do have similarities with others as they are closely related to them.

Figure 2.6 *Different species of woodlice.*

Figure 2.7 *Monkeys, lemurs and tree shrews are all related.*

Selective breeding

Animals and plants of the past were very different from those we see today. Over the years people have tried to breed organisms with special characteristics. So the differences we see are due to a process called **selective breeding**, where organisms with desired characteristics are bred to give offspring which also show the desired characteristics. A new breed of dog, the Staffordshire bull terrier, was produced by breeding together bulldogs and terriers. The Staffordshire bull terrier combines some of the qualities of both bulldogs and terriers. Chance may still affect the results, for example if two champion racehorses mate, their offspring may not be a champion.

Figure 2.8 *A bull dog, a terrier and a staffordshire bull terrier.*

Selective breeding is also important in farming. For example, a farmer may have a cow that produces a lot of milk. He may know of a bull that has fathered cows that produce very creamy milk but not much of it. He can breed the cow and the bull together and hope that the calves will eventually produce lots of creamy milk.

Victoria Savoy Cabbage

Figure 2.9 *A nineteenth century cabbage and ornamental cabbages bred for their colours.*

Summary

- A species is a group of organisms with very similar features that can breed together and produce fertile offspring.
- Variation can be continuous e.g. height, or discontinuous, e.g. blood group.
- Variation between species is greater than the variation within a species.
- Variation can be caused by environmental and genetic factors.
- Closely related species have similar characteristics.

Questions

1 Copy and complete the following sentences. Humans are all different, this difference is called _____. It may be one of two types, _____ or _____. Variation can be caused by genetic or _____ factors.
[Total 2]

2 a) What is variation? *[1]*
  b) Explain the difference between the two different types of variation. *[2]*
  [Total 3]

3 What does the term 'normal distribution' mean?
[Total 2]

4 What are the causes of variation? *[Total 2]*

5 Explain why there is more variation between species than within a species. *[Total 1]*

6 a) What is selective breeding? *[1]*
  b) Why is selective breeding important to farmers? *[2]*
  c) Explain how a farmer would selectivly breed tomatoes to produce plants with the largest yield (i.e. greatest number of tomatoes in a year). *[3]*
  [Total 6]

6.3 Patterns of inheritance

What are genes? Why are they so important? We know that some characteristics of an organism are inherited from its parents. When genes are mixed during sexual reproduction variation occurs.

DNA

The human body contains billions of cells. Each cell has a specific function. Each cell is controlled by its **nucleus**. The nucleus of a cell contains long, threadlike strands called **chromosomes**. There are 46 chromosomes in each human cell. Chromosomes carry pieces of information called **genes**. Chromosomes and genes are made of a large molecule called deoxyribonucleic acid (**DNA**). The DNA molecule is arranged like a twisted spiral ladder called a **double helix**. (A helix is any spiral-shaped object.) Each 'rung' on the ladder consists of a pair of **bases**.

The genetic instructions (blueprint for the body) are carried in the sequenced DNA bases which make up each chromosome. These determine the inherited characteristic of an individual. This information is in the form of a code that controls the order in which amino acids are assembled to produce **proteins**. The proteins are used for the growth of cells and as enzymes that control all the chemical reactions in the body.

Each human cell contains about 2 m of DNA strands forming a double helix.

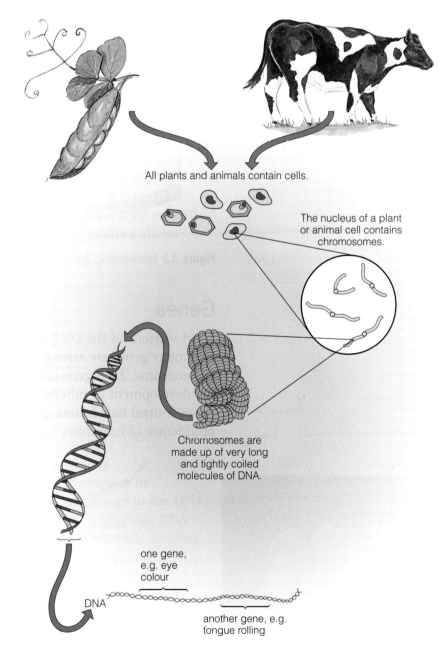

All plants and animals contain cells.

The nucleus of a plant or animal cell contains chromosomes.

Chromosomes are made up of very long and tightly coiled molecules of DNA.

one gene, e.g. eye colour

DNA

another gene, e.g. tongue rolling

Figure 3.1 *Cells, chromosomes and DNA.*

6.4 Evolution

Evolution

How can fossils tell us about the past? Fossils are the remains of plants or animals that lived millions of years ago and are mainly found in rock. They reveal to us small fragments of what happened a long time ago.

Figure 4.1

Fossils

When an organism dies, micro-organisms very quickly begin to decompose the organic material. Fossilisation only takes place under certain conditions which prevent decay occurring. Fossils have been found in the ice of the Arctic, tar pits in the Caribbean, peat bogs of Europe and tree resin. Micro-organisms do not grow well in these environments. Micro-organisms work best where there is oxygen, moisture, warmth and a suitable pH.

A fossil can be dated by looking at the layer of rock in which it is found. Older rocks are usually deeper in the ground, and so contain the oldest fossils. For the exact dating of rock, a process which measures traces of radioactive elements that are in the rock needs to be used. This involves the elements uranium, lead, rubidium and strontium. We can track how organisms have changed over millions of years by looking at fossils.

Figure 4.2 *Fossils in amber and stone.*

> The study of fossils (palaeontology), is thought to have been attributed to a close friend of Queen Victoria, Sir Richard Owen. He invented the name 'dinosaurs' based on two Greek words *deinos* (fearfully great) and *sauros* (lizard). Sir Richard based his study on work that had been carried out by another scientist 15 years earlier. Gideon Mantell wrote about giant fossil reptiles that roamed the earth in the past. The two scientists were working at the same time. Mantell identified the first ancient herbivore reptile, the iguanodon. He thought it must have looked like a 20 m lizard. Owen worked out that the dinosaurs were not all lizard-like and that some stood on legs. The two scientists remained rivals until their deaths.

> In 1986, two archaeologists, Tim White and Donald Johanson, found 302 pieces of a female of the species *Homo habilis* (an ancestor of modern humans). It was 1.8 million years old. It was the first time that bones from the limbs of *Homo habilis* had been found. The specimen was about 1 m tall and far more ape-like than expected!

Conditions on Earth

Conditions on the Earth are always changing. About 3000 million years ago simple unicellular (single-celled) life forms developed. 2000 million years ago worm like animals emerged. 2500–1500 million years ago oxygen was building up on the planet rapidly because of photosynthesising bacteria. The oxygen was poisonous to most early forms of life. As time passed more organisms developed, the landmasses moved and temperatures changed. Only organisms which were adapted to the conditions survived. If

Figure 4.3

they were not adapted to the conditions, they became **extinct**. Biologists believe that by a process of **natural selection** all organisms that exist today have evolved from the first simple life forms. This theory is known as the theory of **evolution**.

Natural selection

All living things have characteristics that help them to survive. Individuals in a species show many differences. This variation is a result of the alleles inherited. There is competition between individuals for food, space and other resources. This leads to a struggle for survival. The individuals which can compete successfully for resources are most likely to survive. This is known as the **survival of the fittest**. If variation gives individuals a greater ability to compete for resources, then the organism will have a better chance of survival, and so live to breed and produce offspring. This ensures that their genetic material is passed on to the next generation.

The result is an organism which is extremely well suited to its environment. The process helps the species become better adapted to survive in its habitat. This process is called natural selection. The inheritance of one small variation will not produce a new species. It is the production of variations over many generations, and their inheritance, that will gradually lead to the evolution of a new species.

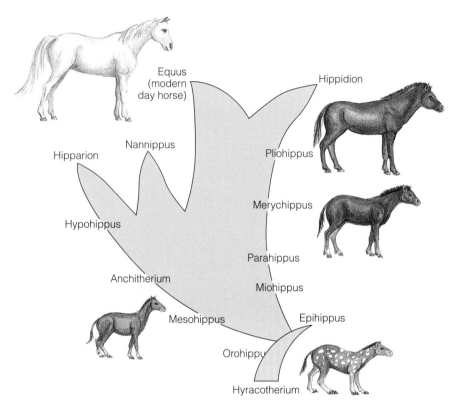

Natural selection often takes place as a result of environmental change. The earliest horses were as small as foxes and lived on wet boggy ground. Their feet had spreading toes that were used for support on the soggy ground. The climate then changed and became hotter. The ground became firmer and those animals that were taller with smaller feet were more likely to survive. This was because they were faster at running away from predators. Gradually, the central toe of the horse became enlarged forming a hoof. This made it easier for the animal to run on firm ground. Over long periods of time changes within a species can produce a different kind of animal. This is an example of evolution.

Figure 4.4 *The stages of evolution of the horse.*

Darwin

In Europe in the 1800s people believed that plants and animals had been made by a creator, God, and had not changed since. In the 1830s, a naturalist, Charles Darwin sailed around the world in a ship called the Beagle, studying plants and animals on different continents. He had different ideas. Darwin collected many samples of fossils. Although the fossils were old, they were similar but not identical to the skeletons of living organisms. Darwin was convinced that the fossils must have been distant relatives of present day animals.

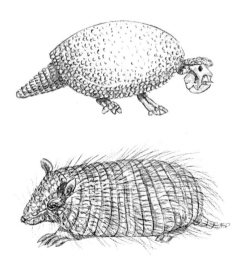

Figure 4.5 *A skeleton of a glytoptodon and a hairy armadillo.*

Darwin developed a theory to explain his observations. He stated that present day animals had descended from those that existed in the past. In 1859 he published a book: *On the origin of species by means of natural selection or the preservation of favoured races the struggle for life*. More simply it was known as *The Origin of Species*. In it, he put forward evidence to support his idea that similar organisms are descended from the same type of ancestor. He also put forward a theory to explain how evolution may have happened. His main ideas were as follows.

- Each species contains a variety of individuals.
- Organisms produce more young than their habitat can support and this leads to a struggle between them for survival.
- Those best adapted to their environment are most likely to survive and breed.
- Organisms pass on to their young the characteristics which will help them survive and adapt to their environment.
- Eventually the organisms may change to form a completely new species.

Summary

- Fossils are the preserved remains of animals or plants which existed millions of years ago.
- Life on earth has been changing ever since it formed.
- Evolution is the slow change of organisms over time.
- Evolution may result in the formation of new species.
- The survival of well-adapted organisms is called natural selection.

Questions

1 Copy and complete the following sentences.
_____ are formed when animal or plant remains are preserved in rock for millions of years. Natural _____ is the process that happens when organisms are best fitted to _____ in their environment. When the _____ changes, failure to _____ results in extinction. _____ is the change in a population over time. *[Total 3]*

2 a) What are fossils? *[1]*
b) List four environments where fossils have been found. *[4]*
[Total 5]

3 List the conditions in which micro-organisms work well. *[Total 4]*

4 What is the theory of evolution? *[Total 3]*

5 Explain the term 'struggle for survival'. *[Total 1]*

6 Explain the term 'survival of the fittest'. *[Total 1]*

7 Why was it significant that Darwin believed that animals had changed over time? *[Total 3]*

History

Carolus Linnaeus (Linne)

Until the eighteenth century scientists in different countries all referred to plants and animals using different names. A Swedish botanist and naturalist, Carl Linnaeus (1707–1778), decided to try to create a system that would make it easier for scientists from different parts of the world to communicate with each other about plants. Linnaeus travelled widely throughout Europe studying and collecting plants. He attempted to classify every known plant and animal. Linnaeus sorted all living things according to similarities in their structure.

In the eighteenth century the most widely understood language among scientists was Latin. So he gave each plant and animal a two-part Latin name. This system is called a **binomial** system. Binomial means two names. The binomial system created by Linnaeus is still used today. Each organism has a genus name that is written with a capital letter and a species name that starts with a small letter. As the name is Latin it is written in italics. Using the binomial system, horses are known as *Equus caballus*. We are known as *Homo sapiens*.

Mendel

Gregor Mendel (1822–1884) was an Austrian monk. He studied mathematics and natural history. Mendel was interested in botany (the study of plants) and wanted to teach biology, but he failed his biology exam twice. He was, however, an excellent mathematician and so taught mathematics and Greek in the local secondary school.

After teaching for a few years, Mendel had to return to the monastery. There he was in charge of the garden. He began to experiment with the plants that he grew. He became interested in how features of pea plants were passed from one generation to another. He monitored the height of the pea plants, blossom colour, position of the flowers on the stem, leaf type, differences in seed colour and shape, and variations in the appearance of the pods. His observations enabled him to suggest how characteristics were inherited. This gave an explanation of how parents pass on their characteristics to their young.

Figure 1 *Gregor Mendel.*

Mendel deduced from his experiments that the characteristics of the plants were controlled by an inherited factor. He worked out and concluded that there were two parts to the inherited factor. One part (or 'particle' as he called them) comes from each parent. It was not until the twentieth century that scientists described these 'particles' as chromosomes and genes.

He worked for eight years carrying out thousands of experiments. He conducted his research in a mathematical way which many people found hard to understand. Some scientists later believed that as Mendel was such a good mathematician he actually fixed some of his results!

Although Mendel published a book containing his ideas, it was not widely read at the time. It was only in the 1900s that Mendel's discoveries became well known when three independent botanists, Carl Corren in Germany, Hugo de Vries in Holland and Erich von Tschermak-Seysenegg in Austria, drew attention to them.

Figure 2 *Pea plants.*

Questions

1 What area of science did Linnaeus study? *[Total 1]*

2 In which century did Linnaeus live? *[Total 1]*

3 What work has Linnaeus been remembered for? *[Total 1]*

4 What sort of naming system did he create? *[Total 1]*

5 What does binomial mean? *[Total 1]*

6 How are living things labelled using this system? *[Total 1]*

7 a) Who was Gregor Mendel? *[1]*
b) What subjects did he study? *[1]*
c) What type of experiments did he carry out? *[1]*
d) Which type of organism did he use as a focus for his experiments? *[1]*
[Total 4]

8 List some of the different characteristics that Mendel monitored. *[Total 4]*

9 Why did some people at the time of Mendel find it difficult to understand the nature of his work? *[Total 1]*

10 What conclusions did Mendel make about inherited characteristics? *[Total 2]*

11 In his findings Mendel referred to particles in the plants. What do we now call these? *[Total 1]*

12 When did Mendel's discoveries become well known? *[Total 1]*

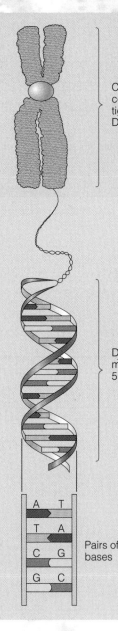

Chromosome consisting of tightly packed DNA thread.

DNA magnified 5 million times.

Pairs of bases

Figure 1 *DNA.*

Applications

Decoding the book of life

In all organisms, the combination of genes that are inherited from parents determine their characteristics. Genes combine to make the **genome** or genetic blueprints of an organism. Each gene is made up of part of a DNA molecule. In 1953, two scientists, James Watson and Francis Crick, established that DNA is made from long strands of chemicals which are coiled together to make a structure called a double helix. The DNA bases are arranged in a pattern that forms a code. The code contains the instructions that make up all living tissue.

Each strand of human DNA can be written down in a code. The code is an arrangement of four letters (bases): A, C, T and G. It has taken scientists almost 50 years, after Watson and Crick first described DNA, to identify the complete code for a human.

The achievement of mapping the human genome was made by scientists working on the project in the UK and the USA. This work could lead to endless possibilities in the field of gene-based medicine. For example:

- personalised medicines – people respond differently to medicines they are prescribed. In the future, individuals could go to the doctor with their own gene map and the doctor would know exactly which medicines to prescribe.
- correcting mutant genes – doctors may be able to correct faulty genes linked to diseases before a baby is born.

The list could go on as gene technology appears to have limitless potential. The use of gene technology raises many important social and ethical questions.

Selective breeding

All living things have characteristics which they inherit from both parents. It is possible to breed new varieties of an organism by taking advantage of variation. Three thousand years ago the Egyptians created wheat from wild grasses.

People often try to breed animals with special characteristics, e.g. horses that can run fast. This is called **selective breeding**. Selective breeding involves selecting a favourable characteristic of an organism and breeding it with another showing a similar feature. The offspring should develop the best features of both parents. These are then bred again with similar individuals until the ideal plant or animal has been produced. Each stage in the selective breeding process is called cross-breeding. Most domestic animals and many fruits and vegetables that we use today are the result of selective breeding. Fruits can be bred which ripen slowly, and that keep well. Animals can be bred to gain weight quickly and have lean meat.

Selective breeding has been very useful in helping farmers produce plants with a bigger yield, which are resistant to disease or drought and which grow quickly. The results have led to great advances in agriculture in many countries of the world.

Selective breeding can also have disadvantages. This is because if you keep cross-breeding animals within the same family you increase the risk of a genetic disease. For example, guide dogs for visually impaired people were bred from a small number of dogs. This is because guide dogs need certain skills, which make them good guide dogs, and these skills were then bred into their puppies. Many dogs which were bred by the Guide Dogs for the Blind Association in the 1980s had the disease PRA (progressive retinal atrophy). This is an inherited disease, which causes blindness in dogs. It was caused by a mutation in a gene which all the dogs had.

Selective breeding can also cause problems because it enhances a certain characeristic. For example Basset hounds have problems with their backs because of their long bodies and short legs. Cows can have problems with swollen udders due to excess milk.

Figure 2

Figure 3

Questions

1 What is a genome? *[Total 1]*

2 a) Who were Watson and Crick? *[1]*
   b) What did they discover? *[2]*
   [Total 3]

3 What is a double helix? *[Total 1]*

4 Explain what you think gene technology is. *[Total 1]*

5 a) What is selective breeding? *[1]*
   b) How long have humans been using selective breeding? *[1]*

   c) Why does selective breeding take such a long time? *[1]*
   [Total 3]

6 Give three examples of the use of selective breeding. *[Total 3]*

7 Why do some people believe that selective breeding is cruel? *[Total 1]*

8 Describe two ways in which selective breeding has improved food production? *[Total 2]*

7.1 Health

How do you keep healthy? Humans are complex organisms. To maintain a healthy body you need to eat the right foods, take some exercise, not take in harmful substances, sleep and be free from disease. Plants need to stay healthy too. They make their own food during the process of photosynthesis. However, they are sensitive to chemicals and pollutants. Plants need the right amounts of water, light and heat to grow healthily.

Maintaining a healthy body is difficult and requires a **balanced diet**. Some adults are extremely overweight or obese because they consume more food than they need. Others may be extremely thin and not consume enough food, because they think they are overweight. There are individuals who abuse their bodies by using drugs and taking risks such as participating in extreme sports. An unhealthy lifestyle can cause illness and damage vital organs in the body.

Diet and exercise

Taking regular **exercise** and eating a balanced diet of different foods helps people become fitter and more healthy. During exercise our muscles work hard. As the muscles work harder more energy is needed. The energy the body needs is stored in food. Energy is released from foods such as sugar (particularly a sugar called glucose), during a chemical process called **respiration**. The word equation is:

$$\text{glucose} + \text{oxygen} \rightarrow \text{carbon dioxide} + \text{water} + (\text{energy})$$

During respiration, the glucose is broken down to release the energy locked in it.

As well as glucose, we also need oxygen for respiration. When we exercise hard we cannot always breathe fast enough to get the oxygen to the muscles in the bloodstream because it is being used up so fast. In fact muscle cells can respire without oxygen for a short time. When this happens, a substance called **lactic acid** is produced in the body and builds up in your muscles. Lactic acid is a toxin and makes the muscles ache. Therefore, after exercising the lactic acid must be broken down. Oxygen is needed to do this. So after exercise you continue to breathe fast and pant to get extra oxygen into the blood to break down the lactic acid.

Figure 1.1 *A balanced body!*

As people do more exercise they get fitter:

- the heart gets stronger and pumps blood more efficiently.
- the lungs get bigger which helps with breathing.
- the body gets stronger and more supple because muscle is built up.

!

During the last 20 years the US Government has found out that the average amount of energy consumed has gone down (i.e. people are eating less). However, they have also found that the number of obese children has risen. It has been suggested that a reason could be a lack of exercise. To help change this situation, health camps for children have been established.

Figure 1.2

Drugs

Drugs are chemicals that change the way the body works. Medicines are drugs that cure illness or ease symptoms. Medicines include painkillers such as aspirin. All non-medicinal drugs affect the workings of the brain and the nervous system. Prolonged use of these drugs can cause unnecessary diseases.

When drugs are taken regularly the body becomes used to the presence of the chemical. The body starts to become **dependent**, that is, it always needs the drug. The person is then **addicted**. If an addict tries to stop taking the drug they can suffer from effects such as sweating, shaking, and feeling sick. These are called withdrawal symptoms.

Drugs that slow down reactions are called **depressants**, and those that make people more alert are called **stimulants**. Caffeine is a stimulant and alcohol is a depressant. Drugs that cause people to see things which are not there are called **hallucinogens**.

Drug	Form	Category	Effect
amphetamine (speed)	pills	stimulant	depression, heart damage
cannabis (marijuana)	smoked with tobacco	hallucinogen	cancer, liver damage
cocaine (crack)	sniffed, injected, smoked	stimulant	brain damage, destroys soft tissue in nose if sniffed
ecstasy	pills	stimulant	confusion, excessive thirst, epilepsy/heart attack
heroin	injected	depressant	highly addictive, liver damage (HIV infection as a result of the use of infected syringes)
LSD	liquid, pills	hallucinogen	mental disturbance, liver and brain damage

Table 1.1 *Some of the common illegal drugs.*

Alcohol

Alcohol contains the chemical **ethanol**. Alcohol gets into the blood through the stomach and then travels to the brain. It is from here that it then affects the nervous system. Alcohol can cause slow reactions and is a **depressant**. People often feel relaxed after drinking alcohol. A large amount of alcohol in the blood can result in people losing self-control and their reactions and judgement are affected. Too much alcohol can also kill you because it depresses the rate of breathing and heart rate.

In most countries it is legal to buy alcohol. However, because of the effect that alcohol has on reaction times, governments set limits on the permitted volume of alcohol in the bloodstream when a person is driving.

The liver breaks down alcohol. One of the major functions of the liver is to remove harmful substances from the body. Excessive drinking can lead to damage and scarring of the liver tissue called **cirrhosis**. People who become dependent on alcohol increase the risk of heart disease, stomach ulcers and brain damage.

Anything you drink may be taken and used in evidence.

DRINKING AND DRIVING WRECKS LIVES.

Figure 1.3

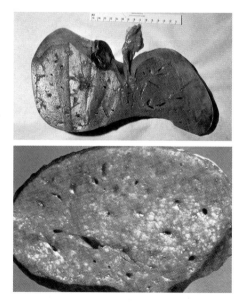

Figure 1.4 *Healthy (top) and damaged (bottom) livers.*

Smoking

Smoking cigarettes is considered to be one of the most preventable causes of death in the United Kingdom. Every year approximately 50 000 women and 70 000 men die of smoking related illnesses.

Cigarettes contain many chemicals such as tar, carbon monoxide, cyanide and the drug **nicotine**. Nicotine is very addictive and that makes it hard to give up smoking. Smokers quickly develop a dependency on nicotine and find it hard to do without it. Nicotine also causes heart disease because it narrows blood vessels in the body. This increases blood pressure, making the heart work harder. Increased blood pressure can also put more strain on the blood vessels, which supply the heart itself with blood.

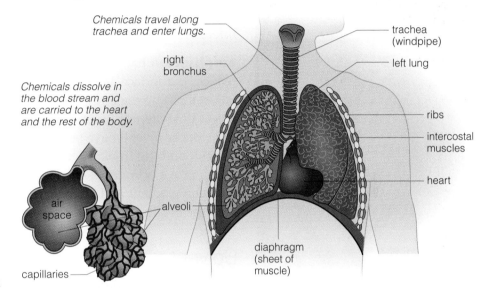

Chemicals travel along trachea and enter lungs.

Chemicals dissolve in the blood stream and are carried to the heart and the rest of the body.

right bronchus

air space

alveoli

capillaries

trachea (windpipe)

left lung

ribs

intercostal muscles

heart

diaphragm (sheet of muscle)

Figure 1.5 *How smoke enters the bloodstream.*

The chemicals in tobacco affect many organs. The **tar** damages the bronchi and alveoli (breathing tubes), and builds up in the lungs. This makes it harder to get oxygen into the blood. The tar can cause the uncontrolled growth of cells in the lung, resulting in cancer. If not treated, the cancer can spread to other parts of the body. Lung cancer or other types of cancer can be lethal so the Government requires the cigarette manufacturers to put a health warning on the packets.

Carbon monoxide from cigarettes stops the blood carrying oxygen efficiently. This puts more strain on the heart, which increases the risk of a heart attack. It combines with the oxygen–carrying substance (haemoglobin) in the blood so that less oxygen can be carried. A pregnant woman who smokes does not give as much oxygen to the baby as normal and the baby, on average, does not grow as much. The 'low birth weight' baby is more likely to get infections in the first few months of life.

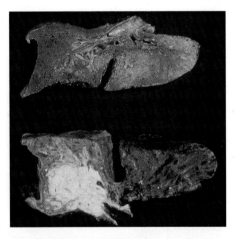

Figure 1.6 *Sections through a healthy lung and a cancerous lung.*

Smokers are also at risk of developing a smoker's cough, bronchitis or emphysema. A smoker's cough happens when the cilia (fine hair like structures in the trachea) are damaged by cigarette smoke and cannot work to remove mucus and dirt from the lungs. After many hours without smoke the cilia start to work and the dirt particles and mucus (a sticky fluid) are removed from the lungs and coughed up.

Bronchitis results when the lining of the trachea and bronchi become sore due to the chemicals in the smoke. They become inflamed and damaged. The air passage gets smaller and it is more difficult to breathe. This causes the difficulty in breathing ('wheezy breathing'). Because the smoke also stops the cilia working, bacteria and dirt particles will be trapped in the mucus but not be removed. The bacteria can cause infections of the lungs like pneumonia or bronchitis.

Emphysema happens when the walls of the alveoli break down, which reduces the surface area. In emphysema the irritated cells in the alveoli are attacked by the body's immune system. The cells are destroyed so bigger holes appear in the lungs. There is a smaller surface area because some of the alveoli have been destroyed. This means that gas exchange is difficult and the smoker gets very short of breath. An emphysema sufferer has to take a cylinder of oxygen with him or her. This will increase the diffusion gradient and help oxygen get into the blood. The oxygen will help the breathing but the damage to the lungs can not be repaired.

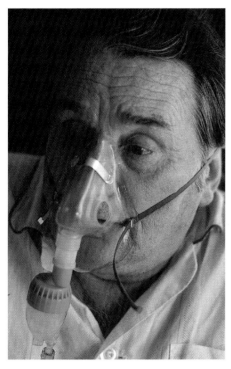

Figure 1.7 *Emphysema sufferers need extra oxygen.*

Solvents

Solvents are substances like glue and aerosols that contain chemicals that release toxic fumes. Solvents are **depressants**. Solvents can be sniffed. The fumes are absorbed into the blood through the lungs and reach the brain. The use of solvents slows reaction times. Solvent abusers who inhale deeply may become unconscious and even die due to heart failure. They can also die of suffocation from inhaling solvents through plastic bags or choking on their own vomit. Solvent abuse can lead to permanent damage to the brain, lungs and liver.

Exercise

When some people with breathing and heart problems visit the doctor, they are not given a prescription for any medication. Instead, after an examination, doctors often now prescribe a course of supervised exercise in a gym.

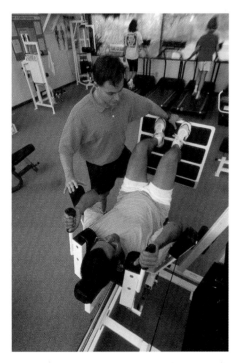

Figure 1.8 *Exercise can replace medication.*

Summary

- A balanced diet is needed to sustain good health.
- Exercise needs energy.
- Energy is stored in food and released during respiration.
- Cannabis, heroin, cocaine and amphetamines are all drugs that can change the way the body works and can damage body organs.
- Drinking alcohol can damage the liver, heart, and stomach.
- Smoking can cause cancer, heart disease and lung diseases such as emphysema.
- The fumes inhaled from sniffing solvents cause lung and brain damage.

Questions

1 Good health is not just the absence of disease it also involves eating a _____ _____.
_____ is used by the body to provide energy. Respiration involves the release of _____ from foods such as sugars. Chemicals that may alter the way the body works are called _____.
The body may be damaged when substances such as _____ are taken excessively. *[Total 3]*

2 How does exercise affect the heart? *[Total 2]*

3 What is the word equation for respiration? *[Total 1]*

4 Name two illegal drugs and in each case state how it could damage your health. *[Total 2]*

5 Suggest ideas why some drugs are illegal. *[Total 2]*

6 Why are cigarettes not sold to people under 14? *[Total 1]*

7 Suggest reasons why people should not drink and drive. *[Total 2]*

8 Look at the apparatus shown in Figure 1.9.
a) Which piece of apparatus represents the lungs? *[1]*
b) What do you think you might see in the piece of apparatus after the cigarette has been finished? *[1]*
[Total 2]

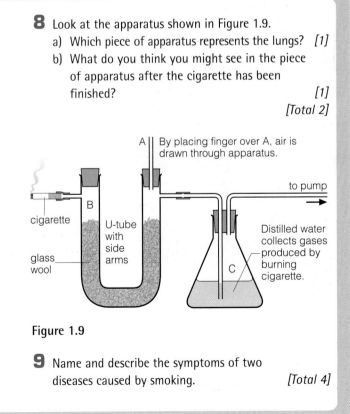

Figure 1.9

9 Name and describe the symptoms of two diseases caused by smoking. *[Total 4]*

7.2 Micro-organisms and disease

How can something that we cannot see cause so much pain and harm? **Micro-organisms** are sometimes called microbes. In the seventeenth century the Dutch scientist Leeuwenhock discovered these 'little creatures'. Two hundred years later the French scientist Pasteur proved that micro-organisms were present in the air, in water and in our bodies.

Pasteur attempted to show that micro-organisms caused decay and that they could invade the body and cause disease. We now know that not all micro-organisms cause **disease**, and not all diseases are caused by micro-organisms. The micro-organisms that do cause disease are called **pathogens**. Some pathogens produce poisonous waste substances called **toxins**.

Micro-organisms

There are four main types of micro-organism:

- viruses
- bacteria
- protozoa
- fungi.

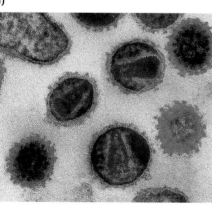

a)

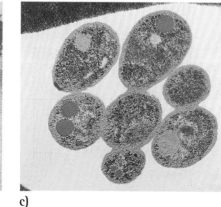

b)

c)

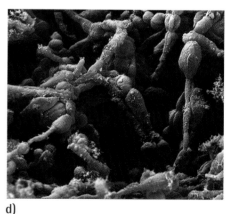

d)

Figure 2.1 a) *A bacterium.*
   b) *A virus.*
   c) *A protozoa.*
   d) *A fungus.*

Viruses are the smallest of the micro-organisms. They can only be seen using the most powerful microscopes. Viruses invade and then destroy living cells. They can only live inside the cells of other living organisms. Viruses are responsible for many diseases, such as: influenza, measles, chickenpox, smallpox and AIDS.

Bacteria are single celled organisms. They are able to live in body tissues between the cells. They need food, warmth and moisture to grow. They can multiply very quickly by cell division if conditions are right. Bacteria cause diseases such as whooping cough, tuberculosis (TB), pneumonia and cholera. *Salmonella* is a bacterium that can cause food poisoning.

Protozoa are single celled organisms like amoeba. They are larger than viruses and bacteria. Protozoa feed by absorbing nutrients from their surroundings. Malaria and amoebic dysentery are caused by protozoa.

Fungi are the largest of the four types of micro-organism. The fungus makes fine threads, which invade cells and absorb nutrients from them. Fungi can live on decaying substances or in living tissue. They include moulds, which live on rotting food. The diseases caused by fungi include athlete's foot, ringworm and thrush.

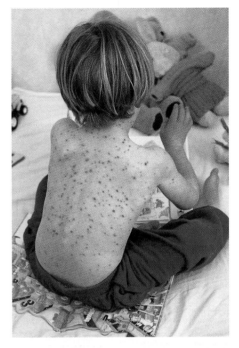

Figure 2.2 *Measles.*

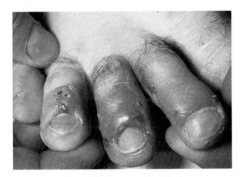

Figure 2.3 *Athletes foot fungus.*

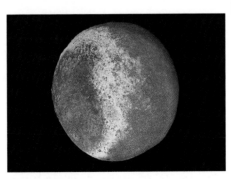

Figure 2.4 *Penicillium mould.*

All individual micro-organisms are very small, but we can see micro-organisms when they are grouped together. A group of micro-organisms is called a **colony**. The blue-green mould that we see on an orange that has gone bad is a colony of *penicillium*.

 Acquired Immune Deficiency Syndrome (AIDS) is caused by a virus called HIV. White blood cells form part of the body's immune system, which defends the body. HIV attacks white blood cells and the immune system stops working. The HIV virus cannot live outside the body. It is passed from one person to another in liquids: semen or vaginal fluids during sexual contact or blood during exchange of syringes when injecting drugs. Using condoms during sexual intercourse and drug users not sharing syringes reduces the risks of contracting AIDS. Currently, there is no known cure for AIDS.

There is some dispute about where the sexually transmitted disease syphilis came from. The general view is that it was brought back to Europe from the Americas by Christopher Columbus. However, there is some evidence (which is disputed), that traces of the effects of syphilis have been found on human remains from the Roman town of Pompeii in Italy.

In the nineteenth century London had three very large outbreaks (epidemics) of cholera. John Snow (who was an anaesthetist) realised that the disease had been caused by contaminated food or drink. He was able to locate the source as a water pump in Broad Street. Snow convinced the authorities to remove the handle of the pump. The epidemic decreased dramatically after that. It was later discovered that the Broad Street pump took water from a shallow well. The water supplying the well had been contaminated with sewage and rubbish.

Spreading of disease

Diseases that are easily passed on are called **infections**. Micro-organisms are passed on from people in a number of different ways. The micro-organisms can get into the body through openings such as the nose or mouth, or breaks in the skin like cuts and scratches.

Method of transmission	Examples
actual contact with an infected person	impetigo, smallpox, blood poisoning (septicaemia), sexually transmitted diseases
contact with an infected person's belongings	athletes foot, ringworm
droplets in the air, coughs and sneezes	influenza, tuberculosis, measles, chickenpox
contaminated food, prepared unhygienically	typhoid, food poisoning
contaminated water, which has been in contact with sewage	typhoid, cholera
carried by animals	malaria, bubonic plague, salmonella, rabies

Table 2.1 *How some diseases are spread.*

Controlling disease

The spread of many diseases has been reduced by the control of micro-organisms. Many diseases in the world are spread through contaminated water. On a small scale, washing your hands after using the lavatory and before handing food can cut down the spread of infections. However, clean water is essential to life. When water becomes contaminated with sewage, diseases such as cholera may be caught. Water can be made safe by treating it with a process of filtering, chlorinating and purification. This is a large scale, expensive process.

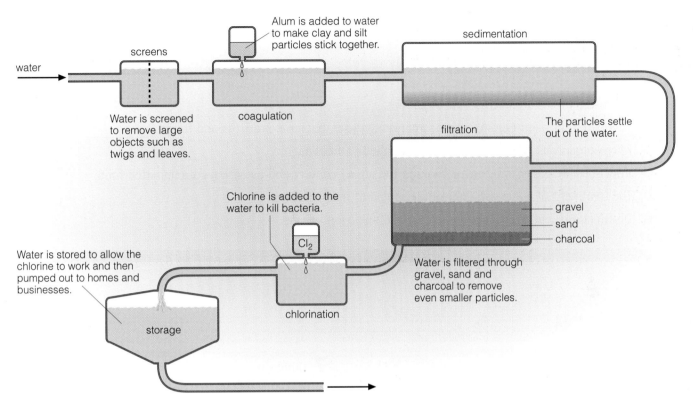

Figure 2.5 *How our drinking water is treated.*

The spread of micro-organisms can also be controlled with the use of chemicals. **Disinfectants** are strong chemicals. They are corrosive and contain chlorine, for example bleach. They kill micro-organisms. Disinfectants can be used in the home. Antiseptics are usually weaker and can be used on the skin. They stop micro-organisms from growing and multiplying.

Antibiotics

The prevention of disease is not always possible. Sometimes medicines are needed to treat disease. A group of medicines that have been very successful in treating diseases are **antibiotics**. The mould *Penicillium* is an example of an antibiotic. Antibiotics kill bacteria. They do not damage body cells and work very quickly. Antibiotics have no effect on viruses.

Figure 2.6 *A range of disinfectants and antiseptics.*

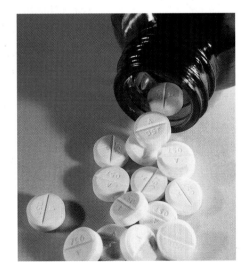

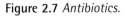

Figure 2.7 *Antibiotics.*

Summary

- Micro-organisms are microscopic organisms.
- There are four main types of micro-organism: viruses, bacteria, protozoa and fungi.
- Micro-organisms which cause disease are called pathogens.
- Infections are easily transmitted through the air, by contact and by eating contaminated food.
- The treatment of water can control the spread of many diseases.
- Disinfectants and antiseptics are used to kill micro-organisms.

Questions

1 Copy and complete the following paragraph. Micro-organisms are everywhere: there are four types, _____, viruses, _____ and _____. Many of them are useful, but some cause serious _____. Viruses are much smaller than _____. They can only be seen with an electron microscope as they are so small. _____ kill bacteria. *[Total 3]*

2 What are micro-organisms? *[Total 1]*

3 What is a pathogen? *[Total 1]*

4 List the differences between fungi and bacteria. *[Total 2]*

5 Design a poster warning people going on holiday of the ways in which diseases are transmitted. *[Total 6]*

6 Explain how can water be made safe to drink. *[Total 4]*

7 Outline the difference between a disinfectant and an antiseptic. *[Total 2]*

8 What is an antibiotic? *[Total 2]*

9 Diphtheria is a bacterial disease. The number of cases reported in England and Wales is shown in Table 2.2.
a) Plot the results on a graph *[3]*
b) Suggest when you think vaccination against diphtheria was introduced. *[1]*
[Total 4]

Year	Number of reported cases in England and Wales
1935	70 000
1940	60 500
1941	61 834
1950	6672
1955	780
1970	4

Table 2.2

7.3 Micro-organisms and food

Can micro-organisms be helpful as well as harmful? Micro-organisms are everywhere. If a micro-organism lands on a surface that has the right conditions for growth, it will multiply quickly. They need food and water to grow and warm conditions. Some micro-organisms are harmful and cause diseases, and others make food go bad. However, not *all* micro-organisms are harmful. Many are used effectively in the brewing, baking and dairy industries.

Food preservation

Bacteria and fungi often spoil our food, making it decay. The micro-organisms produce substances called enzymes that enter the food. The **enzymes** work by breaking the food down quickly. The micro-organisms also produce poisonous substances (**toxins**). These poisons cause us to be sick if we eat the food. The most dangerous bacteria that cause food poisoning include *E. coli*, *salmonella*, and *staphylococci*. To stop micro-organisms from damaging food they need to be killed or the conditions they need for growth must be removed.

One in Three Chickens Contain Salmonella Bug!

E. coli kills yet more

Food Poisoning Strikes Young and Elderly

Soft Cheeses Blamed for Listeria Scare

Figure 3.1 *Food poisoning can affect many people.*

There are a number of different ways to preserve food. The methods chosen will depend on the type of food. Some methods change the taste and appearance of the food. Preservation does not always change a food's nutritional content. Types of food preservation are shown in Table 3.1.

Figure 3.2 *Food can be heat treated, vacuum-packed, dried, canned or frozen.*

Aim	Method	Example
kill micro-organisms – take away oxygen	canning	baked beans
kill micro-organisms – high temperatures or gamma radiation	bottling/sterilisation	baby food
kill micro-organisms – high temperatures 70 °C	pasteurisation	yoghurt, milk
kill micro-organisms – ultra high temperatures 135 °C	ultra-heat treatment	long-life milk
slow growth of micro-organisms – low temperatures 4 °C	refrigeration	meat
stop growth of micro-organisms – very low temperatures –10 °C	freezing	vegetables
slow down growth – remove water	freeze drying	herbs
slow down growth – remove water	smoking	bacon
slow down growth – conditions are changed	preserving adding salt, sugar or acid (vinegar)	fish, jam, pickled onions
stop growth – no water or oxygen	vacuum packing	coffee

Table 3.1 *Types of food preservation.*

Although food can be preserved and stored safely, food poisoning still happens. If people handle food with contaminated hands, do not cook food for long enough or leave food out uncovered, then micro-organisms reproduce rapidly. Food poisoning can be avoided by following good hygiene habits.

Figure 3.3

Uses of micro-organisms

Sewage treatment

Micro-organisms play an important role in recycling chemicals around us, because they can break down waste materials effectively. Raw sewage is treated with millions of micro-organisms in sewage works. The treatment makes the sewage safe enough to be placed back into rivers.

Dairy products

The dairy industry uses micro-organisms to make cheese and yoghurt. They are made by mixing bacteria with milk. Milk contains many micro-organisms. When left, lumps form which are called curds; the liquid part of the milk is called whey. During cheese making, an enzyme called rennin is added to make more curds form quickly. An enzyme is a substance that speeds up a chemical process. The curds are then skimmed off and made into cheese. During yoghurt making the milk is fermented with bacteria.

Figure 3.4 *Cheese being made.*

Antibiotics

The commonly prescribed antibiotic, penicillin, is obtained from a fungus, blue *Penicillium* mould.

Production of alcohol

Yeast is a single-celled organism: it is a type of fungus. Yeast is able to respire with or without oxygen (anaerobically). Yeast feeds on sugar and produces a toxin called ethanol or alcohol. During a chemical process, yeast is added to sugar and to fruit such as grapes to make alcoholic drinks. This process is called **fermentation**. During fermentation the gas carbon dioxide is also produced. If the alcohol content of the drink is too high it kills yeast. Distillation is used to make strong drinks such as whisky and vodka.

Making bread

Yeast is also used in the baking industry. Bread making uses yeast mixed with a little sugar, flour and water to form dough. The yeast respires and the carbon dioxide gas forms bubbles inside the dough that cannot escape. This makes the dough swell and expand. The alcohol that is also produced evaporates when the dough is baked in a hot oven.

Figure 3.5

Single cell protein (SCP)

This is made from the cells of micro-organisms which have been grown to make food for humans or animals. The cells may be grown on waste material, for example, **Pruteen**. It is made by the bacterium *Methylophilus methylotrophus* growing on methanol. Methanol is a waste material which can be made from natural gas. Pruteen is manufactured under sterile conditions.

Another SCP product is **mycoprotein**, which is produced when the fungus *Fusarium graminearum* is grown on waste flour. In fact *Fusarium* will grow on any material containing carbohydrate. It is made into Quorn which is used as vegetarian replacement for meat.

! Micro-organisms are important in the digestive process in many animals. The stomachs of mammals such as cows and sheep contain bacteria that produce very powerful enzymes. The most important enzyme is cellulase. It breaks down plant material such as cellulose so that the animal can absorb the nutrients locked in the material. We have micro-organisms in our gut too which help our digestion and are fed by certain yoghurt drinks.

Figure 3.6

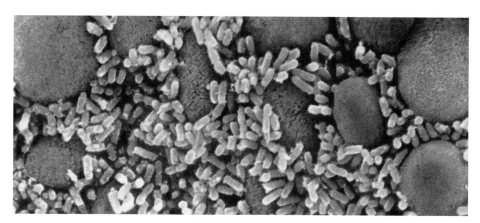

Figure 3.7 *Helpful bacteria that live in your gut. (Bacteria are coloured yellow).*

Summary

- Micro-organisms need food, water and warm conditions to grow.
- The destructive effect of micro-organisms on food can be prevented using preservation methods.
- Micro-organisms are used in many industries including brewing, baking, and dairy.
- Wine, beer, bread and cheese are all made with micro-organisms.

Questions

1 Copy and complete the following sentences.
_____ such as yeast and bacteria can be useful to humans. We make medicines such as _____, drinks such as _____, as well as foods such as cheese and _____. When yeast is added to sugar solution a chemical process called _____ happens. _____ can also spoil food. [Total 3]

2 What conditions do micro-organisms need to grow? [Total 3]

3 Explain how micro-organisms make food go bad. [Total 2]

4 Imagine you are taking part in a 'round the world' sailing race. Suggest what foods you would take and explain why. [Total 4]

5 Why is sugar added to yeast to make alcohol and bread? [Total 1]

6 Some cheeses have holes in them, others blue veins. What could have caused these characteristics? [Total 1]

7 How does cooking help in the prevention of food poisoning? [Total 1]

8 Name one use of a single cell protein (SCP)? [Total 1]

7.4 Immunisation

How does the body protect itself from micro-organisms? Micro-organisms are all around us. The body needs to protect itself in many ways.

Natural defence

The human defence system is often compared to that of a castle. With a castle the first form of defence is the outer wall. If a hole occurs in the wall soldiers work quickly to plug the holes. They are second in the line of defence. If some invaders get through they are then faced with the third form of defence, the inner barricade, which contains highly skilled defenders. The skin is our first line of defence. It acts as a barrier to prevent invading micro-organisms from entering the body. If we cut the skin, the blood produces clots to seal the cuts.

The third line of defence in the body is white blood cells. These deal with the micro-organisms once they are inside. This defence mechanism is called the **immune system**. Sometimes the body's natural immune system cannot deal with all the micro-organisms it encounters and so medicines called **antibiotics** assist the body to fight against the micro-organisms that cause diseases.

As well as the skin and the blood, there are other ways the body can defend itself against disease. For example, our eyes make an enzyme called lysozyme which kills bacteria and prevents eye infections. The acid in our stomach helps to kill bacteria in food.

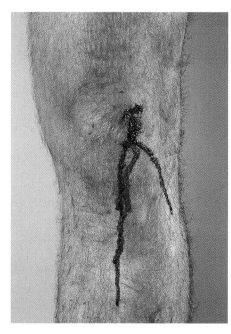

Figure 4.1 *Cuts allow bacteria into the body.*

The immune system

As there are many micro-organisms around us, it is not difficult for them to invade the body. Once they invade, they multiply quickly. The body must react quickly and destroy them. This is the job of the white blood cells. There are many types of white blood cell. The job of some is to search for and recognise the invading bacteria or viruses. This is fairly easy as the invaders (or foreign bodies) have a protein coating which is different from the protein on the surface of human cells. The proteins are called **antigens**.

Some invaders also produce harmful substances called **toxins**. **Lymphocytes** are a type of white blood cell that produce antitoxins to neutralise the toxins. They then produce antibodies. **Antibodies** are proteins that stick to the invading micro-organisms. The antibodies lock onto the antigen and force the bacteria or viruses to clump together.

This action then makes it easier for **phagocytes** (another type of white blood cell) to surround and digest the micro-organisms.

The white blood cells make a unique antibody for each type of invading antigen they encounter. Some antibodies stay in the blood after the bacteria or viruses have been destroyed. This means that if the person is ever infected again by the same micro-organisms the body is already prepared to fight, and extra antibodies are produced very quickly. The body is then said to have **immunity**.

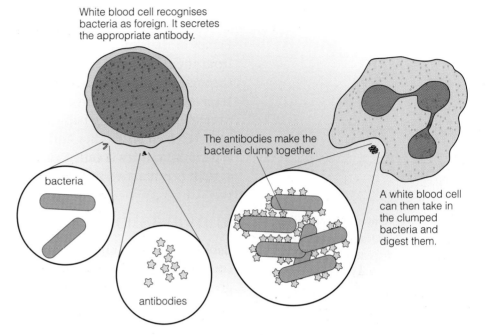

White blood cell recognises bacteria as foreign. It secretes the appropriate antibody.

bacteria

antibodies

The antibodies make the bacteria clump together.

A white blood cell can then take in the clumped bacteria and digest them.

Figure 4.2 *White blood cells destroy bacteria.*

Vaccinations

Doctors can now stimulate a person's immune system before they contract a serious disease. This system is known as immunisation or **vaccination**. Vaccinations are injections that prevent people from contracting some diseases. This method of protection is called artificial active immunity. When a person is vaccinated a vaccine is passed into the blood. Vaccines can be made up of different things:

- dead antigens, e.g. polio
- weak strains of a micro-organism, e.g. TB
- toxins of the micro-organism which have been made harmless, e.g. diphtheria.

These vaccines force the body to make its own antibodies. This results in the body's natural immunity being increased. The white cells in the blood will react quickly to the antigens. This active immunity can protect a person for a long time.

An allergy is an exaggerated immune response. In asthma inflamed narrowed airways create breathing problems. An underlying allergy is often the cause. Hay fever is an allergy to pollen.

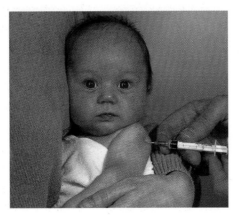

Figure 4.3 *Vaccination helps to protect us.*

Passive immunity

Babies in their mother's womb receive protection against some diseases from their mothers. This is due to antibodies passing from the mother, through the placenta, to the baby. Once the baby is born it still receives antibodies from its mother through breast milk. The protection that young babies have is short lived because they have only received antibodies and have not made any for themselves. This type of immunity is called **passive immunity** as the baby's immune system is not active in the making of antibodies.

Immunisation programme

Babies and young children are very susceptible to diseases. In many countries, individuals are protected against some diseases by being given a course of vaccines at a very early age. The immunity of a young person is then gradually built up. Occasionally the vaccine makes the person feel unwell for a few days.

Age	Immunisation
2 months	triple (diphtheria, tetanus, whooping cough) and polio
3 months	triple and polio
4 months	triple and polio
15 months	MMR (mumps, measles and rubella)
4 years	triple and booster MMR
1 year onwards	meningitis
12-14 years	tuberculosis (BCG)
13 years	rubella (girls only)

Table 4.1 *Typical vaccination course.*

We know that antibiotics kill bacteria and have no effect on viruses. However there are some bacteria that are resistant to antibiotics. Some strains such as *Staphylococcus aureus* are called super-bugs. A super-bug is a bacteria which is resistant to most antibiotics, even methicillin, which is one of the strongest. It attacks wounds and can cause fatal blood poisoning (septicaemia). This strain of *Staphylococcus aureus* is now present in many hospitals.

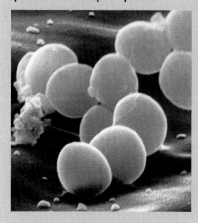

Figure 4.4 *Staphylococcus aureus.*

Summary

- Micro-organisms are everywhere. They are not all harmful. However, if the skin is broken, micro-organisms quickly invade the body.
- The body has many natural protective barriers.
- Many changes take place in the body to kill micro-organisms, e.g. blood clotting, the destruction of micro-organisms by white blood cells, the production of antibodies and the production of antitoxins to neutralise the antigens of the invading micro-organisms.
- Once antibodies have been produced, the body develops a natural immunity to a disease.
- We can be immunised (vaccinated) against diseases. Vaccines contain dead or harmless micro-organisms which are similar to harmful ones.
- Antibiotics are used to help the body fight disease. Antibiotics kill bacteria and have no effect on viruses.

Questions

1 Copy and complete the following sentences. _____ can enter the body through one of many natural openings or a cut. The body has natural defences such as the skin, and _____. Some of these cells can surround _____ and kill them. Other white blood cells produce antitoxins and _____. Immunisation is a way to increase the body's natural _____. This takes the form of a mild dose of a disease being _____ into a person. *[Total 3]*

2 List the natural defences the body uses to keep out bacteria and viruses. *[Total 3]*

3 a) What are antigens? *[1]*
   b) What are toxins? *[1]*
   c) What is the job of antibodies? *[1]*
   [Total 3]

4 a) Why are white blood cells important? *[1]*
   b) Name two different types of white blood cells. Explain what each one does. *[4]*
   [Total 5]

5 How does the clumping of invading micro-organisms help the body defend itself? *[Total 2]*

6 Why is it unlikely that a person will suffer with measles twice? *[Total 2]*

7 a) Explain the difference between active and passive immunity. *[1]*
   b) Explain the difference between natural and artificial immunity. *[1]*
   c) How are babies protected from disease? *[1]*
   [Total 3]

8 Find out why only girls are vaccinated against rubella at 13. *[Total 1]*

7.5 Genetic modification and biotechnology

Can a pig's heart be transplanted into a human? All living things are made up of genes. Genes are sections of DNA. The DNA code is very similar in many organisms. This means that one organism can understand the genes of an other. This makes **genetic engineering** possible.

Genetic engineering

This involves scientists adding genetic material to, taking genetic material away from, or transferring genetic material between organisms. Genes can be cut out of the DNA of one organism using enzymes and then added into the DNA of a bacterium. The added gene is then copied by the bacterium many times.

Insulin is a hormone that lowers the concentration of sugar in the blood. People with diabetes do not produce enough insulin. In the past insulin was taken from the pancreas of pigs (and cows) after they died. This was a difficult procedure. In 1980 doctors in London carried out trials of genetically engineered insulin produced by bacteria. They inserted the gene for healthy human insulin into bacteria. The bacteria then produced lots of human insulin. This is now widely available as humulin (human insulin).

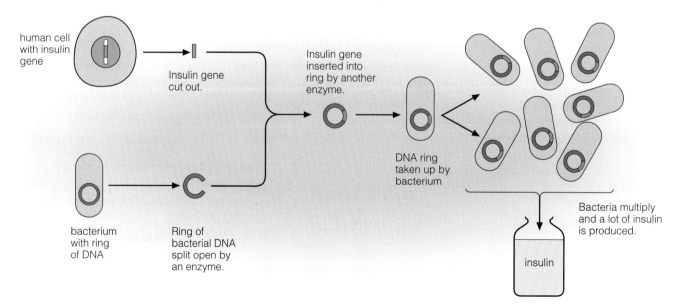

human cell with insulin gene

Insulin gene cut out.

Insulin gene inserted into ring by another enzyme.

DNA ring taken up by bacterium

Bacteria multiply and a lot of insulin is produced.

bacterium with ring of DNA

Ring of bacterial DNA split open by an enzyme.

insulin

Figure 5.1 *Genetic engineering of insulin.*

Cystic fibrosis is a genetic disease, which causes thick mucus to be produced in the lungs and gut. This makes breathing difficult and as the mucus is a good breeding ground for micro-organisms, cystic fibrosis sufferers tend to get lung infections easily. The disease is caused by a faulty gene. Scientists have developed a nasal spray that contains the normal gene, and when it is inhaled it causes the cells in the lungs to make normal mucus.

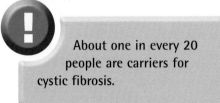

About one in every 20 people are carriers for cystic fibrosis.

Human eggs can be taken out of a woman's body, fertilised and then put back. While the egg is outside the body, theoretically, genes could be transferred to cells so that they produce certain characteristics. This could be used to stop babies being born with the inherited disease cystic fibrosis. However, this has not yet been done in the UK as it is illegal to tamper with the genome.

Cloning

Cloning is a method of reproduction that results in genetically identical offspring being produced. Plants have been cloned for a long time. When plant growers develop a variety of a plant which has features that they want to preserve, they often clone the plant, so that all the offspring have those special features.

British scientists have now developed a method of cloning animals. They first began work cloning frogs, and then in 1997 the first adult mammal was cloned, Dolly the sheep.

Figure 5.2 *Dolly the sheep.*

Dolly the sheep was the first successful clone out of 277 attempts. A skin cell was removed from a fully grown sheep. An egg from another sheep was taken and its nucleus removed to leave just the cytoplasm of the cell. The nucleus of the skin cell was put into the empty egg cell and the whole egg cell was implanted in a third sheep. It grew into Dolly. Dolly is a clone of the sheep that donated the skin cell – this means that the two sheep are genetically identical.

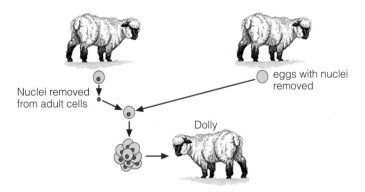

Nuclei removed from adult cells

eggs with nuclei removed

Dolly

The American cartoonist, Joe Babera, does not sign the frames of his cartoons with an ordinary pen. Instead he marks them with his DNA pen. DNA taken from his hair is cloned and then mixed with ordinary ink.

Figure 5.3 *Cloning.*

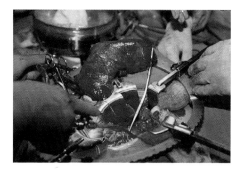

Figure 5.4 *An organ transplant taking place.*

Organ transplants

Today, some people with damaged organs such as a heart, kidney or liver can have them replaced. As early as medieval times transplants of limbs were carried out. Unfortunately there are not enough human organs to supply all the people who need them. It was not until the twentieth century that transplantation became successful. Medicines were developed to prevent the immune system rejecting the new organ. Techniques for matching tissue were also developed so that the implanted organ matched the rest of the body tissue as closely as possible.

Xenotransplantation is a process which uses animal organs. Scientists have been able to modify donor animals genetically by breeding them in a way that enables them to carry a small piece of human DNA, about 1% of the genome. Pigs have been found to be the best choice as their organs are a similar size to human organs. Xenotransplants can also be used on humans with damaged skin. This procedure is called a skin graft. Xenotransplantation is not carried out in the UK because of the risks of transferring diseases from pigs to humans.

Genetically modified food

Genetic modification is a method used where individual genes can be copied and transferred to another living organism. This is done to alter the genetic makeup of the organism. More than 60 plant species have now been genetically modified. Commercial crops such as oilseed rape, maize, potatoes, tomatoes and soya have been modified.

Plants are modified so that they can be resistant to diseases, to improve their nutritional value, or improve their ability to survive in different conditions such as drought, flood or frost. For example, maize has been genetically modified so that it can make a protein from the bacterium *Bacillus thuringiensis*. This protein kills an insect which is a major threat to the maize. Soya has been modified to make it tolerant to certain weedkillers (herbicides). This means that the crop only needs to be sprayed once with the herbicide. Everything except the soya is killed. This means that less herbicide is used by the farmer.

Genetic engineering has many positive uses. It can be used to help produce cures for diseases and can help in food production. If plants are genetically immune to pests then fewer chemicals will need to be used in the countryside. However, there may be many unknown side-effects. The action of removing genes from one organism and putting them into another organism could have unexpected effects. The issue of genetic engineering in embryos is also an issue which raises many ethical and moral questions. It is a subject which will continue to be debated.

Summary

- Genes are sections of DNA.
- Genetic engineering involves the altering of the instructions of a cell.
- Genetic engineering can be used to produce human proteins e.g. insulin.
- Cloning is the process of replicating cells.
- Animal organs can be genetically modified so they can be used by humans.
- Plants can be genetically modified to make them more resistant to pests, diseases and droughts.

Questions

1 Copy and complete the following sentences. All organisms have genes which use the same DNA code. So the _____ from one organism can be used by another. Genetic engineering can involve _____ the genes from the cells of one living thing and _____ them into the cells of another. Genetically identical individuals are called _____. *[Total 2]*

2 What are genes? *[Total 1]*

3 What is genetic engineering? *[Total 2]*

4 a) How can insulin be genetically engineered? *[2]*
b) What are the advantages of using this method? *[2]*
[Total 4]

5 a) What is cystic fibrosis? *[1]*
b) How can it be treated with genetic engineering? *[1]*
[Total 2]

6 a) What is cloning? *[1]*
b) Why are plants cloned? *[1]*
[Total 2]

7 a) After a transplant a patient is given drugs to prevent their immune system working properly. Why do you think that this is done? *[1]*
b) Why is it a potential problem? *[1]*
[Total 2]

8 Waiting lists for organ transplant operations in the UK are growing by 15% a year. How could these lists could be shortened? *[Total 2]*

9 Why is it thought that pig organs can be used in humans? *[Total 1]*

10 What is a skin graft? *[Total 1]*

11 If xenotransplantation is the transplant where the donor organ comes from an animal, suggest a term for a graft where the donor tissue comes from an animal? *[Total 1]*

History

Smallpox and Edward Jenner

Spanish explorers were said to have introduced smallpox into America in the sixteenth century. The native American population was reduced by approximately 6 million people by smallpox after it was introduced to the continent.

Smallpox is a disease that is caused by a virus. The sufferers developed rashes, spots and scabs filled with pus. Pus is a thick yellowish liquid produced by infected tissue. The earliest recorded case of smallpox was in 1157 BC. The mummy of Pharaoh Ramses V showed evidence of smallpox. The Chinese developed a cure in the twelfth century which involved pus being taken from the sores and put up the noses of healthy people. This method, called variolation, gradually made its way to Europe. Variolation did not have a high success rate. In 1729 Lady Wortley Montague was known to have taken the liquid from one of the spots of a person infected with smallpox, and then scratched it into an unaffected persons arm. This was done to give the unaffected person immunity from the disease.

In the eighteenth century, an English doctor, Edward Jenner (1749–1823), noticed that some of his patients, such as milkmaids, who had caught another disease cowpox did not contract smallpox. He began to study agricultural workers who came into regular contact with cows. He found that they were **immune** to smallpox. Jenner discovered that the liquid from the cowpox could protect people from smallpox. He first experimented with a small boy who had never had cowpox. Jenner gave the boy cowpox by putting pus from a cowpox sufferer into cuts on the boy's arm. The child developed cowpox. A few months later Jenner took pus from a smallpox sufferer and placed this into the boy's cuts. The boy did not contract smallpox. He then began to inject people with the cowpox virus. Jenner's work led to the development of a **vaccine** for smallpox.

Figure 1 *A cartoon of Edward Jenner at work.*

However, in the nineteenth century many people were still dying from smallpox: 60 million people died in Europe. People were unsure about the use of vaccines, and only the rich could afford to be vaccinated. By the twentieth century the number of people dying from smallpox was falling but 15 million people in the world still died from the disease. In 1947, there was a smallpox epidemic in New York. As a result, the health authority decided to vaccinate every citizen in New York. In that year, 7 million citizens of New York were vaccinated against smallpox.

In 1947, the World Health Organisation (WHO) stated that they were going to **eradicate** smallpox by the twenty-first century. They concentrated their effort in a ten year plan, which employed over 200 000 health workers in 40 different countries. The numbers of people dying from smallpox decreased dramatically. The last person to die from smallpox was recorded in 1977. So in 1980, WHO announced that the world was free of smallpox. A triumph for modern medicine.

The story does not end there. Although people are not dying from smallpox, the virus is still on the planet. Samples of the virus have been kept. It is thought that governments keep samples which can be used in biological warfare.

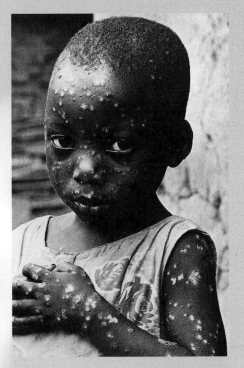

Figure 2 *A child with smallpox.*

Questions

1 What causes smallpox? *[Total 1]*

2 What are the symptoms of smallpox? *[Total 1]*

3 Why were so many Native Americans killed by smallpox? *[Total 2]*

4 a) Who was Edward Jenner? *[1]*
   b) What work did Jenner pioneer? *[1]*
   [Total 2]

5 a) What is variolation? *[2]*
   b) When and where was it invented? *[2]*
   [Total 4]

6 How was smallpox eradicated? *[Total 2]*

Applications

Biosurgery: nature's healers

In the twentieth century antibiotics were used a great deal to treat wounds. But in the past maggots were used instead. Maggots were used by the Aborigines of Australia, the hill people of Burma, Europeans, and the Mayans of South America to treat wounds.

A surgeon, Baron Dominique-Jean Larrey, serving with Napoleon in the 1820s invented the field ambulance. He recorded in his diary how soldiers with maggot infested wounds would arrive at his tents already showing signs of recovery. William Baer, a surgeon in World War I, described a situation where he saw two soldiers on the battlefield who had maggots in their wounds for several days, but these men had no fever or infection. The maggots were protecting the soldiers from diseases such as tetanus and septicaemia and at the same time healing their wounds by eating the rotting tissue.

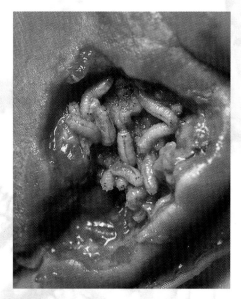

Figure 1 *Maggots cleaning a wound.*

After World War I, in 1929, Baer began trials using blowfly maggots to treat wounds. His results were very good. He then began to cultivate blowflies to use their eggs. By the 1930s maggot therapy, as it was called, was also being used in Canada and the USA in more than 300 hospitals. With the discovery of antibiotics, by the end of World War II, penicillin was used on a large scale to treat wounds. Maggot therapy virtually disappeared.

In the 1980s and 1990s it has been found that bacteria are becoming increasingly resistant to antibiotics. Super-bugs such as methicillin resistant *Staphylococcus aureus* (MRSA) are causing severe problems preventing wounds from healing. Maggots can achieve naturally what artificial medicines are failing to do. In 1990, an American doctor, Robert Sherman, noticed healthy infection-free tissue in a leg wound crawling with maggots. He set up an insectary to breed maggots for use in hospitals in California. He conducted trials and showed that larva therapy, as it is now called, increases the rate of healing of pressure sores. It is also more cost effective than treatment with surgery and antibiotics. Although maggot therapy is effective many health professionals are reluctant to use the method.

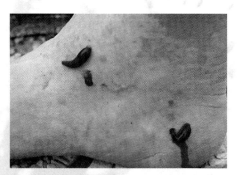

Figure 2 *The saliva of leeches improves blood circulation*

Maggots are not the only creatures to be used in biosurgery. Leeches are also used. Leeches have suckers that suck blood. They were used as early as 200 BC for the purpose of blood letting by healers. By the nineteenth century this practice had become unfashionable.

Currently patients who have lost an ear or a finger may find that leeches have been attached to their wound. This happens where poor circulation of the blood or blood clotting threaten a re-attached ear or finger. The natural anticoagulant in the saliva of the leech improves the blood circulation. Even when the leech has had its fill of blood and falls off, the patient continues to bleed for up to 10 hours. This stops clotting of the blood and allows the small capillaries to develop.

> Honey can be used to help in the healing of wounds. When honey is placed on wounds it competes with bacteria for moisture, and so helps speed up the drying out of the infected wound.

Food

Different micro-organisms have been used as sources of food for many years. The alga *Spirulina maxima* was eaten by the Aztecs. It is now used as a food supplement and is added to health drinks. Mycroprotein is a product which is derived from the mould *Fusarium* which grows on carbohydrates like potatoes. The mould is high in protein and low in fat, as a result it is collected, processed and made into a meat substitute (see Section 7, chapter 3).

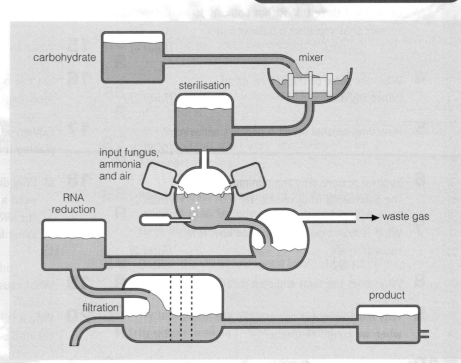

Figure 3 *How mycroprotein is made.*

Questions

1 Which peoples have used maggots in healing?
[Total 3]

2
a) Who was Baron Larrey? [1]
b) What did he realise? [1]
c) Who was Williams Baer? [1]
d) What was his contribution to medicine? [1]
[Total 4]

3 How many establishments around the world were using maggot therapy by the 1930s? [Total 1]

4 Why did maggot therapy die out after World War II? [Total 1]

5 What other organisms have been used in biosurgery? [Total 1]

8.3 Human influences

Figure 3.1 *Indian tiger.*

How have we changed our environment? Humans have been on the Earth for the last 2 million years. They have interacted with the environment in the same way as all other species. However, in recent years, the effects of humans on the environment have been increasing.

Competition for space

In many regions of the world the human population has increased so much that the original habitat has been destroyed. Humans are winning the competition for space. Species like the Indian tiger are restricted to smaller and smaller areas. The population has decreased to a few individuals and by 2020 it is likely to be extinct.

To grow more food people cut down forests (**habitat destruction**) and use the land for crops or grazing. Unfortunately, the area of destroyed forest was home to a great many different types of plants and animals. If the whole population of one species is lost permanently we say that the species has become **extinct**. Some plants and animals from endangered habitats have been found to contain chemicals that could be useful to humans. For example, an anti-cancer drug has been extracted from the leaves of the Madagascan periwinkle.

By the year 2000, 24% of the land surface had been covered by arable crops or by towns. 26% is used for grazing.

Competition for space can be seen if too many animals are grazed in one area. **Overgrazing** occurs and plants cannot re-grow. When there are too few plants the soil is eroded more easily. Normally, plant roots hold the soil together. Heavy rainfall may wash the soil away or it could dry out and be blown away by the wind.

In the UK, 90% of the population is urban and this means that less space is available for plants and animals. The area around housing is compacted or covered in concrete so that the original inhabitants cannot live there. Having many buildings also causes problems with drainage of rainwater. Soil will absorb rainwater but concrete will not. The water runs into rivers faster and rivers flood more often (Figure 3.3). The planners try to understand the systems and build in measures to protect areas which humans value.

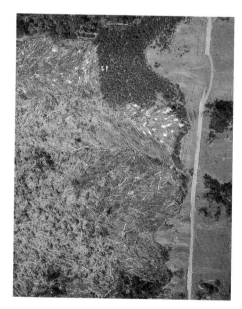

Figure 3.2 *Forest habitat destroyed during felling.*

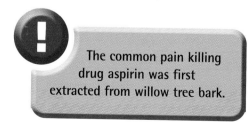

The common pain killing drug aspirin was first extracted from willow tree bark.

Figure 3.3 *Flooding caused by unusually high rainfall and good drainage from built-up areas or farmland, October 2000.*

Sometimes human influence can help a species. The presence of buildings has created new habitats for animals. Bats may live in roofs instead of caves or trees. The use of salt on the roads in winter to keep them free of ice has let seaside plants grow along the roadside (Figure 3.4).

Competition for resources

The work involved in obtaining the raw materials for our lifestyle causes damage to the environment. An open-cast mine is a visual eyesore and the dust, noise and road or rail network to transport people or products all reduce the ability of other organisms to live around the mine. Dust falls on the plants and stops some of the light getting to leaves. The plants are weakened and are more likely to get diseased just as we are when we breathe in dust.

Figure 3.4 *The seaside plant thrift growing by a roadside away from the sea.*

Climate change

Non-renewable sources of energy like coal, oil and uranium are being used to power our lifestyle (Figure 3.5).

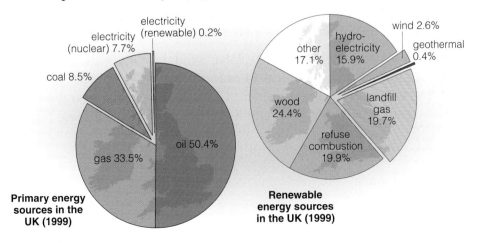

electricity (renewable) 0.2%
electricity (nuclear) 7.7%
coal 8.5%
oil 50.4%
gas 33.5%

Primary energy sources in the UK (1999)

other 17.1%
hydro-electricity 15.9%
wind 2.6%
geothermal 0.4%
wood 24.4%
landfill gas 19.7%
refuse combustion 19.9%

Renewable energy sources in the UK (1999)

Figure 3.5 *Renewable energy sources have less effect on the environment but only provided 0.2% of the electricity in the UK 1999.*

Burning fossil fuels produces carbon dioxide, which may be causing climate change. Carbon dioxide is also produced when forests (biomass) are cut down and burnt. Felling forests also means that there are fewer large plants absorbing the carbon dioxide in photosynthesis. All of this means that carbon dioxide is building up in the atmosphere.

Together with methane (a waste gas from cattle digesting their food), the carbon dioxide absorbs the heat given off from the earth. This makes the atmosphere warmer and is called **global warming**. Even a small increase in global temperature could have a large effect. For example:

- wind and rainfall patterns may change
- ice caps may melt, increasing the sea level
- sea levels could also rise because water expands when it is warmer.

By the year 2100 it is predicted that the sea level will rise between 9 cm and 88 cm and the average global temperature will rise between 1.4 °C and 5.8 °C

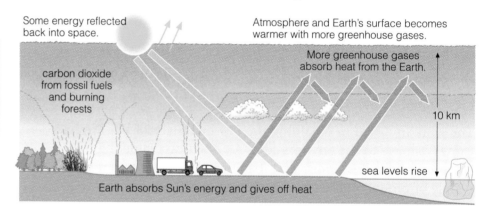

Figure 3.6 *Greenhouse effect mechanism.*

Scientists are not sure if global warming is taking place or not but there is more and more evidence that it is happening. Many people are very worried about these changes. In England and Wales nearly 2 million properties are at risk from river and sea flooding.

About 27% of coral reefs have died or have suffered serious damage. By 2025 half of the coral reefs will be lost due to higher sea temperatures and other pollution from humans.

If renewable sources of energy like solar, wind, moving water or replanted forests were used instead of fossil fuels then humans would have less effect on the environment. However, renewable energy sources tend to be less reliable and less efficient than fossil fuels.

Figure 3.7 *Coral reefs are under threat from global warming and pollution.*

The ozone layer

The ozone layer high in the atmosphere stops damaging radiation from the sun getting to the Earth's surface. The ozone layer is being destroyed by a group of substances called chlorofluorocarbons (CFCs). CFCs are man-made molecules, which were used in aerosols and fridges. The chlorine in the CFCs enters the upper atmosphere and reacts with ozone to destroy it. This is most noticeable above the Antarctic where it is described as an ozone 'hole'. The extra radiation, which reaches the earth through the thin ozone layer, could cause skin cancer in humans as well as harming all other organisms.

Acid rain

The waste gases from burning fossil fuels also contain sulphur dioxide and oxides of nitrogen. These gases dissolve in water in the atmosphere to form acid rain. Buildings are damaged by the acid. Plant leaves will not photosynthesise properly because the acid in the leaves stops the chloroplasts working properly.

When acid rain runs into ponds or lakes many animals cannot survive. Fish get oxygen from water through their gills. The gills are very delicate and if the water becomes acidic, the fish produce extra mucus on the gills as protection. The mucus means that the fish cannot get as much oxygen from the water and they die. Many lakes in Scandinavia have become crystal clear because there are no plankton (microscopic plants and animals) living in the water.

Figure 3.8 *Helicopter spreading lime on a acid lake to neutralise it.*

Pesticides and bioaccumulation

Pesticides are chemicals that kill pests such as slugs, insects or rats. Some pesticides are designed not to chemically break down. Wherever the pesticide ends up in the ecosystem, animals are likely to be affected by the poison.

A pesticide may be sprayed onto plants to kill pests. The plants are eaten by herbivores. The herbivore often stores the poison in fat which it does not use regularly. As the pesticide is not broken down, it will be transferred into the next animal in the food chain. The animal in the next trophic level has to eat many smaller organisms in order to get enough energy to survive. It takes in the stored pesticide from each of its food organisms. The pesticide becomes more concentrated. The process is called **bioaccumulation**. The top predators accumulate so much pesticide that it harms them so they may not be able to breed.

The poison DDT was used widely after the World War II to kill mosquitoes which carry malaria. DDT is not broken down in the environment and it has entered food webs all over the world. It has even been found in the penguins of Antarctica. It was responsible for the death of many predators like the peregrine falcon. The falcon nearly became extinct in the UK.

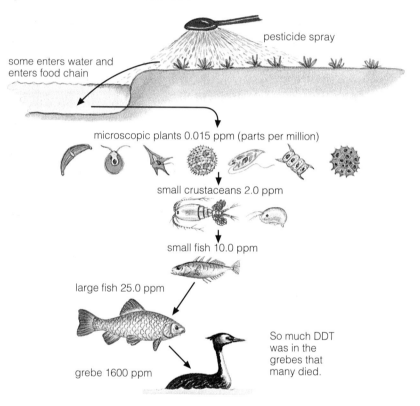

pesticide spray

some enters water and enters food chain

microscopic plants 0.015 ppm (parts per million)

small crustaceans 2.0 ppm

small fish 10.0 ppm

large fish 25.0 ppm

grebe 1600 ppm

So much DDT was in the grebes that many died.

Figure 3.9 *Bioaccumulation of DDT in the community around Clear Lake, California.*

Pollution from accidents

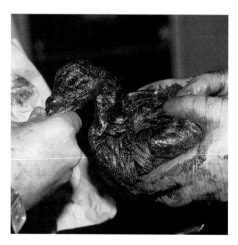

In 1967, the first major oil tanker disaster occurred. The Cornish coast was covered in thick oil from the stricken oil tanker, Torrey Canyon. The birds for example, cormorants, living in the area got covered in oil. The feathers lost their waterproof layer. The birds could not keep warm and died. Many other marine organisms also died, but after 10 years there was little sign of the disaster. Micro-organisms started to decompose the oil and much of it was hidden underneath sand or somewhere under the sea. The process is slow but the natural ecosystem has returned.

Figure 3.10

Toxic minerals from mines may be accidentally discharged into rivers. The minerals kill most of the organisms in the river because they interfere with enzymes in their cells. All organisms are affected. The mining of precious metals or those needed in industry can have a great cost to the environment.

In January 2001, a dam burst at the Aurul gold mine in Romania. The water released contained cyanide at a concentration of up to 700 times acceptable levels. Once it entered the River Tisza, the effect on wildlife was disastrous. Virtually all organisms in the river were killed, from algae, to fish and otters, and there were fears that the cyanide would enter the food chain. Over a thousand tonnes of dead fish were removed from the river in the first two weeks following the spill. The extent of the disaster was so great that local people declared the river to be 'dead'. The flow continued from Romania, into Hungary and onto Serbia, by which time it had been diluted to near normal levels.

The accident threatened the drinking supplies of over 2.5 million Hungarians and the livelihoods of 15 000 fishermen. Environmentalists have warned that it will take between ten and twenty years for the river ecosystem to recover. However, it is feared that some species of fish may never return.

Figure 3.11 *River pollution from a copper mine in Spain.*

Sustainable development

The overgrazing and pollution examples given earlier in the chapter show the way humans change the environment for the worse. The effects usually destroy part of an ecosystem. Sustainable development means continuing to improve and develop standards of living for all people without using up all the Earth's natural resources. For example, we should

- use energy from renewable resources, e.g. wind power and solar cells
- make housing and transport more energy efficient
- use items made from replanted forests
- make sure that mines or any environment that has been changed is renovated after use into productive areas
- recycle all waste substances.

All the living things around us must be respected and conserved. The great diversity of organisms must be protected as each has a part to play in the development of each community. Some of the currently rare species might be useful to humans in the future. Zoos are important in maintaining breeding programmes so that animals can be returned to natural habitats. Other conservation measures include the protection of habitats by creating nature reserves or national parks which help to limit the activities of humans.

! The National Parks cover 13 740 km², which is 9% of the land in England and Wales.

Summary

- Some animals are becoming extinct because their habitats are being destroyed.
- Some species which can live around humans are increasing.
- Increasing carbon dioxide levels are associated with climate change.
- The ozone layer is being damaged and this could lead to more cases of skin cancer.
- Acid rain is caused by pollutants from fossil fuels.
- Pesticides can accumulate in the food chain so the top predators are accidentally killed.
- Many human activities produce accidents which damage the environment e.g. oil spills.
- Sustainable development means continuing to develop higher standards of living without destroying the Earth's resources.

Questions

1 Copy and complete the following sentences. Human populations are _____ and require extra space to live. New farmland is made by _____ forests. The Indian tiger will become _____ because of habitat destruction. Much of the _____ needed in the developed world comes from _____ sources like coal and _____. Oil spill accidents kill many birds.
[Total 3]

2 List four effects on the environment of the human population increase.
[Total 4]

3 Give two examples to show that human activity has increased space where they can live.
[Total 2]

4 What is the difference between a renewable and non-renewable resource?
[Total 1]

5 How does dust from mining affect:
 a) plants
[1]
 b) animals like humans.
[1]
[Total 2]

6 How does carbon dioxide warm the atmosphere?
[Total 1]

7 Explain how the warming of the seas has an effect on humans?
[Total 2]

8 Give two different problems caused by deforestation.
[Total 2]

9 a) Why is acid rain a problem for plants?
[1]
 b) Explain why fish can die if the water becomes too acid.
[1]
[Total 2]

10 a) Why do pesticides accumulate in organisms?
[1]
 b) What is meant by bioaccumulation?
[1]
[Total 2]

11 Give two reasons why many seabirds die when there is an oil spillage in their habitat.
[Total 2]

12 Explain the idea of sustainable development.
[Total 2]

13 Why are zoos important?
[Total 1]

14 Write a short paragraph on each of the following points to explain how the action is polluting the environment:
 a) burning fossil fuels
[3]
 b) using CFCs
[3]
 c) deforestation.
[3]
[Total 9]

History

Ecology and populations

Ecology is the science studying the interactions between organisms and their environment. Ecology started as the study of natural history.

Humans have always needed to know which other organisms are around them for food. They must also be able to avoid predators. Some types of organism could be used for medicine. Humans have tried to modify some species to cultivate them. Others have been domesticated. Working with the many different species gave us the idea that population numbers did not change very much. Nature was in balance.

However, sometimes there were plagues. Food production by farming had supported more people but occasionally one species became out of control. In the 4th century BC Aristotle tried to explain plagues of field mice and locusts by saying the mice reproduced much faster than could be destroyed by their natural predators. Aristotle stated that only heavy rain could make the mouse plague disappear. At the time a plague was thought to be a punishment from God. Plagues were uncommon. Most of the time the numbers of each species remained the same as nature was balanced. People thought that extinctions did not occur.

By the mid 18th century the philosophers writing about natural history continued to support the ancient ideas. The Comte de Buffon published many volumes of a Natural History from 1749. The volume in 1756 argued against the ideas of Aristotle. Buffon wrote about many agents of destruction for each species understanding that predators and disease prevented population increase. Buffon argued that shortage of food and disease stopped the mice plagues, not heavy rains! He said that rabbits would reduce the countryside to desert if they were not eaten by foxes and birds.

The most famous theory on population was written by Thomas Malthus in 1798 and was called 'An Essay on the Principle of Population'. Thomas Malthus was interested in history and economics. At the time that he was writing, Britain was going through a time of industrial growth, but for most people the standard of living was not improving.

Malthus thought that the human population increases faster than we can increase the food supply. He predicted that the shortage of food would always cause war, famine and disease. Malthus suggested that the 'lower classes' should have less children so there would be more food to

Figure 1 *Thomas Malthus (1766–1834).*

go round. This idea was not popular. Normally families would be large so that the children could work and provide money for them all.

Agriculture and medicine have improved a lot since Malthus wrote his essay. They have allowed people to survive longer. Families do not need to be so large. The world population is increasing very quickly but there are still areas of famine in the world today.

Malthus' ideas also had an important effect on Charles Darwin. Darwin read the essay and realised that in a large population many individuals would compete for the limited resources. There will be a struggle for survival. This was one of the ideas on which he based his theory of evolution.

Scientists following on from Malthus used mathematical equations to describe population growth. In 1838 the S-shaped growth curve was described by Verhulst but the importance of his work was not recognised until the 20th century. Other scientists described the balance between the birth and death rates in mathematical terms. These ideas are still used by ecologists to predict population numbers today.

Questions

1 How did Aristotle think that a plague of mice was stopped? [Total 1]

2 What factors did Buffon think stopped the plagues? [Total 2]

3 What factors did Malthus say limited the increase of human populations? [Total 3]

4 Which famous scientist used Malthus's idea of population growth? [Total 1]

5 Malthus said that the human population increased faster than food supply increases. If a population of one hundred increased by 10% a year and their food supply increased by 10 tonnes per year the data shown in Table 1 are obtained.

a) Plot these data with both lines on the same graph. [5]

b) What trend does the graph show? [2]
[Total 7]

Year	Population	Food produced (tonnes)
0	100	100
1	110	110
2	121	120
3	133	130
4	146	140
5	161	150
6	177	160
7	194	170
8	214	180
9	235	190
10	259	200

Table 1

Applications

Farming techniques and productivity

In some areas of the world crops can grow but their growth is limited by lack of water or poor soils. People use the plants to feed their animals. They use the milk produced for food and later kill the animal for meat. The number of links in the food chain is three: plant to cow to human. In this food chain the cow has used up much of the energy originally trapped by the plants. If people ate the plants the transfer of energy would be more efficient.

In Britain animals are reared in intensive farming systems. The farmer tries to keep the energy losses to a minimum. If the chickens or pigs are kept in small pens then they cannot move around as much. They do not use as much energy. If the pens are indoors in heated houses then the pigs will not need to use as much energy to keep themselves warm. Both these factors mean that the farmer does not have to buy as much food for the pigs. The animals use more of their food for growth. It is the growth of the meat that is important for the farmer. He can sell the animal at a profit. The cost of heating fuel is cheaper than the extra feed needed by the animals.

Many people object to these intensive farming practices. They say the animals are not treated in a humane way. They believe animals should have a life similar to free animals in the natural world. Farmers look after the animals and want to keep the animals in the best health. They get the most money for the healthiest animals because they have usually grown quickest. The debate between the groups continues.

Figure 1

Figure 2 *Intensive farming of pigs.*

Is the earth a giant spaceship?

In Arizona, USA, an enclosed system called Biosphere 2 was built in the 1980s for people to live in. It was sealed from the outside world and only had sunlight as an energy input. After several months they began to run out of oxygen and the food production was not as much as expected. The best efforts of the scientists were not good enough.

Scientists have studied the ecosystems on the Earth but have not been able to copy them. What is so special about the Earth? It only receives the light and heat from the sun. No other extra-terrestrial being comes and gives the earth a regular clean out!

The idea that the earth is a self-sustaining 'spaceship' was put forward by James E. Lovelock as Gaia hypothesis. (Gaia was the Greek earth goddess.) He suggested that the organisms on the Earth were able to regulate their environment so that changes were not so noticeable. Some scientists disagree with this idea.

The many incidences of pollution mentioned in this section show that ecosystems are affected by human activity. However, over the age of the Earth these changes are usually local or going to affect humans more than the other species.

Figure 3 *Biosphere 2.*

Questions

1 What do you understand by areas of the world which are 'more productive'? *[Total 1]*

2 Give two reasons why plants might not grow well. *[Total 2]*

3 Suggest why animal products give a better balance to the diet than plant products only. (you may need to look at Section 2, chapter 3). *[Total 2]*

4 Give two ways in which intensive farming increases the growth rate of animals. *[Total 2]*

5 Discuss with others the advantages and disadvantages of intensive farming and then create lists. *[Total 6]*

6 Why was Biosphere 2 built? *[Total 2]*

7 What type of organism produced the oxygen in the atmosphere? *[Total 1]*

8 a) Where did the name Gaia come from? *[1]*
   b) Try to explain what the Gaia hypothesis is. *[4]*
   [Total 5]

Questions

1 a) Put the following organisms into the correct order in the food chain. *[1]*

caterpillar sparrowhawk oak tree blue tit

b) Draw a pyramid of numbers for the food chain. *[1]*

c) The pyramid of biomass for the food chain is a regular pyramid. Explain why the shape of the number pyramid is different. *[1]*

[Total 3]

2 Bats can live in caves. They fly out of the cave at night to catch insects. They produce droppings, which are a food source for many organisms. Figure 1 shows part of the food web for the organisms living in and around the cave.

a) In summer, birds enter the caves and eat many of the beetles. Suggest why the population of millipedes might:

i) increase

ii) decrease. *[2]*

b) Name one herbivore from the food web. *[1]*

c) Name one parasite from the food web. *[1]*

d) Name three predators from the food web. *[3]*

e) Use the information in the question to work out the feeding level of the beetles. *[1]*

f) Draw the pyramid of numbers and biomass for the following food chain. Estimate the width of the feeding levels. The relative shape is important not the actual number or mass.

flowering plants → moths → bats → fleas *[4]*

[Total 12]

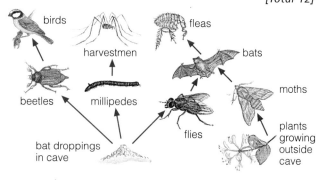

Figure 1 *(not to scale).*

3 Figure 2 shows what happens to most of the energy in the food that a bullock eats in one year.

a) State the word equation for respiration. *[1]*

b) Calculate the total energy which remains in the body of the bullock. *[1]*

c) What is this energy used for? *[1]*

d) Suggest two different ways that a farmer can reduce the energy lost by each bullock as 'thermal transfer'. *[2]*

e) Suggest a reason why reducing the 'movement and thermal transfer' losses are cost effective for the farmer. *[1]*

[Total 6]

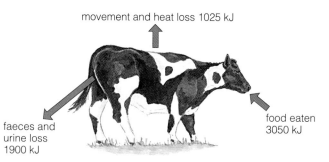

movement and heat loss 1025 kJ

faeces and urine loss 1900 kJ

food eaten 3050 kJ

Figure 2

4 The growth curve of a population sometimes forms an 'S' shape. Sketch the population graph and explain why each part of the graph has a different slope. *[Total 5]*

5 a) Predict how overgrazing will affect the numbers of plants, other herbivores and predator populations within one season. Give a reason for each prediction. *[6]*

b) Suggest what might happen after 2 years. *[4]*

[Total 10]

6 A gardener always grew lettuces every year and he noticed the snails feeding on them. He also found piles of snail shells where he saw thrushes perching. He counted the number of snails and different thrushes in the garden over several years. Figure 3 shows the pattern he obtained.

a) What was the maximum number of snails in year 2? [1]

b) In which year were there most thrushes? [1]

c) Suggest why there were more thrushes in year 4 than in year 2. [1]

d) Write out the simple food chain from the information given. [1]

e) Draw a pyramid of numbers for the food chain. [1]

f) Suggest two reasons why the number of snails did not increase every year. [2]

g) If the gardener used a pesticide to kill the snails, suggest what would happen to the thrushes, giving your reasons. [2]

h) Explain why pesticides are often considered pollutants in the environment. [1]

[Total 10]

7
R Find out about the food web in an aquarium. How may it differ from the examples in this section?

8
R Study an area near to your home over a year e.g. a hedgerow, garden, or pond. Record the different types of animals visiting the area. Record the days when leaves and flowers are first seen. Work out a food web for the area.

9
R Find out what went wrong in Biosphere 2.

10
P What factors would affect time of leaf growth in oak trees of a small wood?

11
P What factors would affect the growth of yeast cells in a laboratory beaker?

12
P Peacock butterfly caterpillars feed on nettle leaves. How would you investigate the effect of peacock butterfly caterpillars on the growth of nettles in the laboratory or green house?

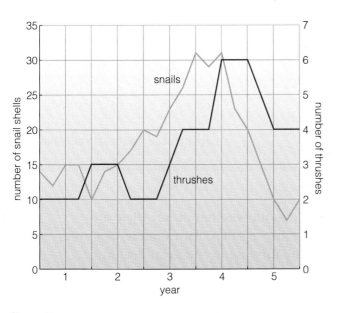

Figure 3

9 Investigations

The purpose of an **investigation** is to find the answer to a question. For example a scientist might ask 'Does exercise increase the heart beat rate?'. When you are doing an investigation you must test your question so that you can come to a conclusion.

New ideas are developed and tested in science all the time. Eventually if an idea is well tested it may be accepted as fact. However, even well established facts can sometimes be proved to be wrong by further experiments or new ideas.

Variables, values and relationships

When you exercise many different factors affect your body. These are called variables. Each variable is described in words or numbers with units which are called values.

Variable	Value
sex	male, female
age	between 11 and 14 years
mass	between 25 and 70 kg
time for exercise	30, 60, 90, 120 s
rate of exercise	number of step-ups per second
Heart beat rate	between 60 and 180 beats per minute

Table 1

Investigations involve finding out whether or not there are relationships between different variables. For example, does the amount of exercise affect the increase in the heart beat rate?

The variable changed by the scientist is called the **input variable** (or independent variable). In this example, the time of exercise would be the input variable. The variable which is affected by the change is called the **outcome variable** (or dependent variable). In this example, the heart beat rate would be the outcome variable.

Fair testing

To find out about the effect of one input variable any other possible input variable must be kept the same. In this example, where a scientist is investigating the effect of length of exercise period on the heart beat rate, to make it a fair test, the same rate of exercise and the same sex and age group of people must be used.

Carrying out investigations

When you do an investigation it is important to plan and carry out your experiment as accurately as possible. The instructions shown below will help you to make sure that you have not forgotten anything.

Plan

1 Make observations and think about the subject. Describe briefly what you are trying to find out. This is the aim.
2 List all the variables that might affect the outcome variable.
3 Choose one variable to investigate – this is the input variable.
4 Make a prediction about the effect of the input variable on the outcome. Try to explain why you think that this will happen using your scientific knowledge.
5 Plan how to carry out the investigation. Make it as accurate as possible. Remember to think about repeat readings. Draw a diagram of the apparatus and make an equipment list.
6 Say how you will make it a fair test.
7 Describe how you will make it safe.
8 Show the plan to your teacher.

Obtaining evidence

9 Do the experiment.
10 Record the results in a table.

Analysing and considering evidence

11 Describe the pattern shown by the results (you may need to plot a graph first).
12 State the conclusion of the experiment and try to explain in scientific terms why this happened.

Evaluation

13 Evaluate the investigation. This means that you should decide how good your experiment was, how reliable the results are and how you could improve it if you did it again.

An example investigation

The first step is to be sure of the idea that you are investigating. Your teacher will usually give you guidance. It is based on making observations and asking questions. This example uses a fieldwork investigation. This is slightly different from a laboratory experiment because the manipulation of the input variable has been done by 'the environment' already. Your job is to choose the places to measure the effect keeping all the other input variables the same.

Plan

What you have to do.

1 Make an observation or read about a process. Think about what you want to find out. Write down the aim of the investigation.

2 List all the variables that could affect the outcome variable.

3 Choose one variable to investigate – the input variable. Write down the input and output variables. Write down how you will keep all the other variables the same.

An example from a pupil.

A muddy path goes across an area of the school playing field. Why don't the plants grow in the middle of the path? Some types of plants cannot grow where there is too much trampling. The soil might be damaged or the leaves damaged when trampled. I want to find if the amount of trampling stops all the plants growing.

There are several things that could affect where plants grow:
- *the arrival of seeds*
- *the time allowed for the growth of the plants*
- *availability of water*
- *availability of light*
- *availability of nutrients in the soil*
- *the temperature*
- *amount of damage from trampling*
- *frequency of mowing.*

I shall investigate the effect of trampling on where the plants can grow. The input variable is the amount of trampling. The output variable is the number and type of plants growing at a spot.
The path was chosen so that there were no trees or bushes within 10 m of the observation place. This makes sure no other plants were taking the nutrients or sheltering the path from rain and sunshine. Each sampled part had been cut at the same time. The grass had been sown more than 5 years ago so the plants had had the same chance to grow.

4   Make a prediction about the effect of the input variable on the outcome variable. Try to explain why you think this using your scientific knowledge. Do not worry if your prediction is wrong as the point of an investigation is to find out the truth.

The greater the amount of trampling (nearer the middle of the path) then the fewer plants will be found there. The plants cannot grow because shoes damage the plant leaves. They cannot photosynthesise and so the grass plants don't get the energy they need to grow. Different types of plant have different reactions to the trampling. Some can survive better than others because their leaves are tougher.

5   Plan how to carry out the investigation. Choose and list the apparatus you will use and state how much you need to vary the input variable (a minimum of five values is needed). You may need to try a couple of the values to see if the method works and you can measure the results. Consider if you need to repeat any of the observations. A diagram of the apparatus may be needed to show how it is put together and used.

I shall estimate the ground cover of the grass as a transect across the path. The transect will go for 3 m each side of the centre of the path. This is because the boys and girls only walk three abreast which covers about 2 m. A sample will be taken every 0.5 m so there will be six readings on either side of the path centre. The sides of the transect are the controls where there is no trampling.

The quadrat area will be 50 cm by 50 cm. I will estimate the amount of grass in each quadrat as a percentage. I will record both sides of the path and check the results by doing a second transect a little further along the path.

Apparatus
- *0.5 × 0.5 m quadrat*
- *10 m tape measure*
- *2 pegs to hold tape in position*
- *clipboard for recording results*
- *plant identification sheet.*

6   Describe how you will make it a fair test.

To make this a fair test I will
- *use the same size of quadrat each time*
- *measure on both sides of the path*
- *be consistent in estimating the percentage coverage of grass.*

7   Describe how you will make it safe.

To make the investigation safe, I will wash my hands carefully when I have finished.

8   Show your plan to your teacher.

Obtain evidence

9 Do the investigation. Carry out all your experiments as accurately and carefully as you can. If there are any changes to the planned method they must be written down.

10 Record the results in a table. As you record the results think if any of them do not follow the same pattern. Repeat all or some of your measurements. Check you have written down the units you have used. Make sure they are the same for each input variable.

The quadrat was divided into 100 small squares so that it was easier to estimate how much was bare ground or covered by grass. The estimate was accurate to the nearest 5% as some of the small squares were only partly covered with grass and I estimated if it should be counted or not. There were no other types of plants in my quadrats so all the results are only for grass. A tape measure let me position the quadrat at exact distances away from the path centre.

Figure 1

Cover of grass plants (%)						
Distance from centre of path (m)	0–0.5	0.5–1.0	1.0–1.5	1.5–2.0	2.0–2.5	2.5–3.0
left side	0	10	30	80	85	85
right side	0	0	40	85	50*	85
repeat left side	20	20	50	90	95	100
repeat right side	15	20	45	85	100	100
average	9	12	41	85	93	92

Table 2 *Percentage cover of grass across a path.*

* This result was not included in the average as it did not fit the pattern of the others.

Analysis

11 Use the average data to plot a line graph (line of best fit which can be straight or a curve) or bar chart. Always put the input variable along the bottom and the outcome variable up the side of the graph. Describe any pattern shown by the graph.

More people walk in the middle of the path than further onto the field. The amount of grass increases further away from the centre of the path. After about 2.0 m the amount does not increase much more. There is always some bare ground. I did not see any other types of plants where we measured.

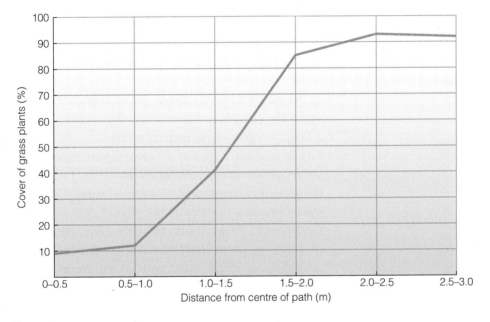

Figure 2

12 State the conclusion from the experiment. Remember that this is a simple statement of what you have found. Try to explain in scientific terms why this happened. Does the conclusion agree with the prediction? Use your science to **explain** the results.

The greater the trampling the less grass was able to grow. If there is little trampling there is still some (about 10%) bare ground.

I predicted that more trampling would stop the plants growing. This is what I found out but there were some in the area that did manage to grow. Also some areas did not have every bit of soil covered by grass. This might be because the roots were competing for water or nutrients. Although the leaves did not cover the soil there could not be any more plants growing at that point. Many of the leaves by the path had dirt on them which could stop photosynthesis. The damage to the leaves could explain the lack of growth.

13 Evaluation

In the evaluation you must think about how good the experiment was. You should think about:

⦿ how good was the experiment?

I think that the experiment was successful because the amount of grass varied as I predicted. The accuracy of estimating the cover of the grass was sufficient for this comparison but was only estimated to the nearest 5%. The graph produced a smooth curve. The method allowed me to identify points that did not fit the trend.

⦿ how could the method or any other part of the investigation have been improved?

I could have improved the measurements if I had taken 100 points for each sample where the divisions of the quadrat I used crossed. At each point I could say if the grass leaves were there. This would give me a better accuracy (1% instead of 5%).

I could also have tried to do more repeats to check the reliability of my conclusion. However, further on the ground is wetter and the path is wider. This would not be a fair test as the ground dips slightly for the water to drain into this area. The reason I chose the repeat transect position was because the ground appeared to be the same as the original.

⦿ were there any results that did not fit in with the others (anomalous results)? If there are any, try to explain why they happened.

The percentage cover of grass on the right of the path from 2.0 to 2.5 m was much lower than expected. At this point there was a very soft patch which was always wetter. The grass does not seem to grow well if the soil is too wet. I did not include this point in my average.

⦿ are the results good enough to be certain about the conclusion?

All the results show the same pattern so I am confident of my conclusion. I am not sure of the reason why the plants cannot grow under trampling.

⦿ can you suggest a further experiment to help answer the original aim?

I could try to find out how much trampling affects the grass. I could count the number of people who walk on the different parts of the path to make the analysis quantitative.

Glossary

abiotic factor   A non-living feature of the environment, e.g. temperature.

absorption   The movement of substances into the body.

active transport   Moving chemicals across a membrane against the concentration gradient, using energy.

adapted   Changed to adjust to new conditions. Organisms adapt to changes in their environment.

aerobic respiration   The release of energy using oxygen.

alveolus   Bubble-like structures in the lungs where gas exchange between the air and the blood occurs.

amino acid   Proteins are made of amino acids.

amylase   An enzyme which breaks down starch.

anaerobic respiration   The release of energy without oxygen.

angina   A type of heart disease causing pain in the chest when the person over-exerts themselves.

antagonistic pair   A pair of muscles which work in opposite directions to each other, e.g. biceps and triceps.

artery   Thick, muscular-walled blood vessel which carries blood away from the heart.

asthma   Condition where breathing is difficult.

atria   Chambers at the 'top' of the heart which blood flows into first.

auxin   Plant growth substance which allows a plant to respond to light.

axon   The long fibre which carries impulses in a nerve cell.

balanced diet   A diet containing all that is needed by a person in the amounts needed.

bile   A substance produced by the liver which helps separate fats into tiny droplets in the small intestine.

bioaccumulation   Increase in the concentration of substances along a food chain.

biomass   The mass of living material.

biome   An area of the Earth which has a particular type of vegetation.

biosphere   The part of the Earth where living things can exist.

blood   Fluid containing cells, that carries substances around an organism.

blood vessel   Tube to contain the blood as it flows around the body.

bronchi   The branches of the windpipe taking air into each lung.

bronchiole   Fine branching tube taking air to all parts of the lungs.

capillary   Tiny blood vessel between arteries and veins which allows exchange of substances between the blood and tissues.

carbohydrase   An enzyme which breaks down carbohydrates.

carbohydrate   Chemical made up from carbon, hydrogen and oxygen atoms – used for energy by organisms.

carnivore   An animal that eats other animals.

cell   The basic unit from which living things are made.

cell membrane   A structure which surrounds the cell and controls what goes in or out.

cell wall   Structure surrounding plant cells giving support. Made of cellulose.

cellulose   A chemical found in plant cell walls. A type of carbohydrate made from glucose.

characteristic   Feature of an individual.

chlorophyll   A chemical that traps light energy for use in photosynthesis.

chloroplast   A structure in plant cells where photosynthesis takes place. Contains chlorophyll.

chromosome   Long strand of DNA found in the nucleus of a cell.

cilia   Small hairs on the surface of some cells. They can be waved to keep mucus moving over the cell surface.

circulation system   The organ system that carries substances around the organism.

community   A group of organisms of different species that live together in one habitat.

cone cell   A cell found in the back of the eye which allows the eye to see in colour.

consumer   An animal that eats another organism.

contraceptive   Method of preventing a woman from becoming pregnant.

cytoplasm   The jelly-like substance that fills a cell and contains most of the cell's chemical reactions.

deciduous woodland   An area of trees which all lose their leaves in winter.

decomposers   Fungi and bacteria which break down dead material.

deficiency disease   A type of disease caused by the lack of a substance in the diet.

diabetes   A disease in which the body cannot control the level of sugar in the blood.

diaphragm   A dome-shaped sheet of muscle which separates the thorax from the abdomen. When it contracts a person breathes in.

diffusion   The process where particles mix with each other without anything moving them. The particles move randomly from areas of high concentration to areas of lower concentration.

digestion   The chemical breaking down of food.

digestive system   The organs where digestion and absorption of food occur.

DNA   Deoxyribonucleic acid. The chemical that contains the genetic code for each individual.

ecosystem   All the organisms and the way they interact with the physical environment in which they live.

egestion   The removal of undigested food from the gut.

endoskeleton   A skeleton which is inside the body and is used for support and protection.

environment   The surroundings in which an organism lives.

enzymes   Chemicals which speed up chemical reactions in cells.

epidermal cells   Layer of lining cells on the outside of leaves.

epithelial cell   Specialised lining cell.

essential amino acid   An amino acid which cannot be made by humans and must be taken in through the diet.

exoskeleton   A skeleton which is outside the body and is used for support and protection.

extinct   When a species dies out completely.

faeces   The undigested food at the end of the alimentary canal that is got rid of (egested).

fats   Chemicals that are used to store energy in organisms.

fermentation   The breakdown of sugar by micro-organisms without the use of oxygen.

fertilisation   When male and female sex cells join together.

fibre   The part of food that cannot be digested.

food chain   The sequence of organisms through which energy flows.

food web   A number of interconnected food chains.

gamete   Sex cell. Either egg or sperm.

gas exchange   The movement of gases between the air and the blood in the lungs.

gastric juice   The fluid released into the stomach containing enzymes.

germination   When a seed starts to grow.

global warming   The increase in the average temperature of the air around the world.

glucose   A simple sugar formed by plants during photosynthesis and used as an energy source in both animals and plants.

habitat   A region of the environment where a particular type of organism lives. Each habitat has a particular group of animals and plants.

haemoglobin   A chemical which carries oxygen in the red blood cells. It gives the blood its red colour.

heart   Organ that pumps blood around the body.

herbivore   An animal that eats plants.

heredity   The passing on of genetic characteristics.

hibernate   To spend the winter in a resting state when the body temperature is much less than the normal active temperature.

hinge joint   A joint that allows movement in one direction.

homologous pair   Pair of chromosomes carrying the same type of genes.

hormone   Chemical that co-ordinates body processes.

immune system   The system which protects the body from disease.

immunity   The body's defence against disease.

ingestion   The taking in of food into the mouth.

inherited characteristic   Genetic feature which has been passed on to an individual from his or her parents.

input variable   The factor which is fixed by the investigator in an experiment.

insect pollination   The transfer of pollen from anther to a stigma by insects.

insulin   A hormone made in the pancreas, which controls the amount of sugar in the blood.

invertebrate   Animal with no backbone.

inverted pyramid   A pyramid of numbers which is upside down.

iris   A layer of coloured tissue found at the front of the eye.

joint   A part of the body where bones join together.

key   A biological table or chart that helps in the identification of living things.

kingdom   Largest group that living things are sorted into, e.g. the animal kingdom.

lactic acid   A chemical produced in muscles when they work without enough oxygen.

lens   Part of the eye behind the pupil, which focuses the image on the retina.

ligament   A tough band of fibres which joins bones together in a joint.

lipase   An enzyme which breaks down fats into fatty acids and glycerol.

lymphocyte   A type of white blood cell that produces antibodies which fight disease.

marrow   Soft substance in the cavity of bones.

meiosis   Cell division which happens when sex cells are produced.

membrane   A thin skin or outer surface of a cell.

menstrual cycle   A series of events lasting about 28 days happening in the female reproductive system. The cycle includes the production of an egg cell and the lining of the uterus to being replaced.

menstruation   When the lining of the uterus and a little blood pass out of the vagina as part of the menstrual cycle.

mesophyll   Tissues in the middle of a leaf which carry out photosynthesis.

micro-organism   An organism which can only be seen by using a microscope.

microvilli   Small finger-like structures on the surface of the vili which increase the surface area of the small intestine even more.

mineral salt   Soluble chemical needed by plants and animals in small amounts.

mitochondria   Structures in the cytoplasm of cells where respiration occurs.

mitosis   Cell division that happens when organisms are growing or replacing cells.

mucus   Sticky fluid.

multicellular   Made of lots of cells.

mutation   A change in the genetic code.

natural selection   When organisms which are best adapted to their environment survive to pass on their genes to their offspring.

nectar   A sugary substance that attracts insects to plants.

nerve ending   The end of a bundle of nerve cells.

nicotine   An addictive chemical found in tobacco.

nucleus   Structure which contains DNA and controls the cell.

oesophagus   Part of the alimentary canal which connects the mouth to the stomach.

oestrogen   A sex hormone that helps to control the menstrual cycle and maintain female characteristics.

omnivore   An animal that eats both plants and animals.

organ   A structure that carries out one or more functions in the organism. It is made of different tissues.

organ system   A collection of organs working together to do one type of function in the organism.

organelle   Structure in the cytoplasm of a cell which can carry out special tasks.

organism   A living individual. The organism must be able to do the seven life processes.

osmosis   The process of the movement of water from an area where there is more water to an area where there is less water through a selectively permeable membrane.

ossicle   Small bone in the middle ear.

outcome variable   The factor which is measured in an experiment.

ovary   Female reproductive organ. Produces egg cells in plants and humans.

overgrazing   When too many animals are eating the plants in an area.

oviduct   Egg tube.

ovulation   Release of an egg cell from an ovary in women.

ovum   The female sex cell (plural: ova).

oxygen debt   The amount of extra oxygen needed to remove chemicals produced during anaerobic respiration.

pacemaker   Area of the heart which controls the rhythm of the heart beat.

palisade cell   Rectangular cells found near the upper surface of a leaf. They contain most of the chloroplasts.

pancreas   An organ which produces digestive enzymes and releases them into the small intestine. It also produces insulin.

pathogen   Micro-organism that causes disease.

penis   An organ in the male which is used for reproduction and the removal of urine.

period   Another term for menstruation. When the lining of the womb is lost with a little blood, through the vagina.

peristalsis   The process of moving something along a tube by a wave of contraction passing along the length.

permanent vacuole   Structure in plant cells containing a solution of sugars, salts and water.

petal   Brightly coloured and/or heavily scented part of a flower which attracts insects.

phagocyte   A type of white blood cell which engulfs and destroys invading micro-organisms.

photosynthesis   The process of forming sugars from carbon dioxide and water using light energy.

phototropism   Growth response of a plant to light.

phyla   The first subdivision of the organisms in a kingdom.

pinna   The outer flap of the ear.

pituitary gland   Small gland at the base of the brain.

placenta   An organ which attaches to the inside of the uterus and allows the fetus to collect food and oxygen form the mother, and get rid of waste.

plasma   Fluid portion of the blood which carries all the other parts of the blood.

platelet   A type of blood cell that helps the clotting of the blood.

pollen tube   Tube that grows from a pollen grain down through the stigma and style and into the ovary.

pollination   Transfer of pollen from an anther to a stigma.

population   Group of individuals of one species in an area.

pregnant   When a woman has an embryo growing inside her uterus.

primary consumer   Animals that eat producer organisms.

producer   A plant which gets its energy from sunlight. They are the starting point for a food chain.

progesterone   A sex hormone that is found in women and prepares the reproductive organs for pregnancy.

protease   An enzyme which breaks down proteins into amino acids.

protein   Chemicals made from chains of amino acids. They are used for growth and repair by the body.

pseudopodia   Feet like protrusions of single celled micro organisms.

puberty   Time when physical changes happen in the body between the ages of about 11 and 15.

pupil   The part of the eye that lets light enter.

pyramid of biomass   The shape describing the mass of individuals at each link in a food chain.

pyramid of numbers   The shape describing the numbers of individuals at each link in a food chain.

receptacle   Base of a flower.

recessive   An allele which codes for a characteristic but can be hidden by another allele.

red blood cell   A specialised cell, full of haemoglobin, which carries oxygen in the blood.

reflex action   An action which does not need conscious thought.

reflex arc   A shortened nervous pathway.

respiration   The process of the release of energy in cells.

retina   The light sensitive layer at the back of the eye.

ribcage   Structure formed by the ribs, breastbone and backbone.

rib muscles   The muscles which move the rib cage up and out when breathing in.

rod cell   Receptor cell in the retina which operates in low light conditions.

root hair cell   Specialised plant cell for absorption of water and minerals from the soil.

saliva   The fluid released into the mouth to start digesting food.

saprobionts   A micro organism that feeds on dead matter.

scrotum   The bag of skin that contains the testes.

secondary sexual characteristic   Characteristic such as developing breasts in females and facial hair in males, which develop at puberty.

selective breeding   Breeding plants and animals to obtain desired characteristics.

self-pollination   The transfer of pollen from anther to stigma in the same plant

semen   A mixture of sperm cells and fluids released by men during sexual intercourse.

semi-circular canal   Structure in the inner ear which helps to detect changes in balance.

sensory cell   Cell which can detect changes in the body.

sepals   Small green leaves used to protect the flower in bud.

septic   Poisoning in a wound caused by the breakdown of cells by certain bacteria.

sexual reproduction   Producing new organisms by combining a male and female gamete.

skeleton   A hard and supportive framework of bones found in vertebrates.

small intestine   A long, coiled section of the gut where the majority of the digestion and absorption of the food occurs.

solvent   The liquid that has dissolved a solid to make a solution.

species   A group of individuals that can reproduce to form fertile offspring.

sperm   The male sex cell (gamete).

sperm duct   Tube that carries sperm from the testes to the urethra.

stamen   Male reproductive organ found in flowers. It is made of an anther and a filament.

starch   A complex carbohydrate which is stored by plants as an energy supply.

stigma   Part of the female part of a flower. It is where the pollen lands.

stimulant   A drug which speeds up the nervous system.

stimuli   A change detected by a receptor.

stomach   A bag like structure to temporarily store food eaten and start to digest the food.

stoma   Pores in the leaf surrounding by two guard cells. Allow air to get into the leaf plural stomata).

stroke   A blood clot in the brain.

sugar   A simple compound formed in photosynthesis. It tastes sweet and can dissolve in water.

support   To carry part of the weight.

synapse   The junction and gap between two neurones.

synovial fluid   Fluid which lubricates joints.

taste buds   Cells which can sense food in the mouth.

testes   Plural of testis. Produce sperm cells.

testosterone   Male hormone.

thyroid   Large gland in the neck.

thyroxine   The main hormone produced by the thyroid gland. It controls the reactions in cells.

tissue   A group of the same cells all doing the same function.

tissue culture   A procedure used in genetic engineering.

tissue fluid   The liquid which bathes the cells. It comes from the blood.

toxin   A poisonous substance.

transpiration   The evaporation of water from a plant.

transpiration stream   Movement of water through a plant from roots to leaves and loss from the leaf.

trophic level   A single stage in a food chain.

tropism   Growth responses by plants

umbilical cord   Carries food, oxygen, and waste between the placenta and the growing fetus.

urethra   Tube leading from the bladder to outside the body.

uterus   Organ in females in which a baby develops.

vaccination   The injection of a very mild dose of a disease to encourage the build up of antibodies.

vaccine   A mild dose of a disease which may be injected into people to protect then against disease.

vagina   Tube in females. The penis is placed here during sexual intercourse.

values   The amount of a factor.

valves   Structures in veins or the heart which stop the blood flowing backwards.

variable   A factor which affects the relationship between two things.

variation   Differences between living things.

vein   Blood vessel which carries blood back to the heart.

ventilation   The taking in and pushing out of air from the lungs. - Breathing.

ventricle   Thick muscular walled chamber of the heart which pump the blood to the organs of the body.

vertebral column   Another term for the spine.

vertebrate   An animal with a backbone.

vesicle   Structure in the cytoplasm where food can be stored or other chemicals broken down.

villi   Tiny finger-like structures in the small intestine which increase the surface area for absorption of the food into the blood.

virus   A micro-organism which is smaller than bacteria and causes disease.

vitamins   Chemicals needed by a person in small amounts to keep healthy.

white blood cell   Cells which fight disease and are found in the blood.

wind pollination   The transfer of pollen from anther to stigma with the aid of the wind

xylem vessel   Specialised cell to carry water and mineral salts in a plant.

Index

Index